FOUR
PLAYS

By CHARLES BUSCH

FOUR PLAYS

By CHARLES BUSCH

The Fireside Theatre

GARDEN CITY, NEW YORK

Design by Maria Chiarino
Photographs by T.L. Boston
Logo Designs by B.T. Whitehill
Manufactured in the United States of America

Quality Printing and Binding by
BERRYVILLE GRAPHICS
P.O. Box 272
Berryville, VA 22611 U.S.A.

"THE LADY IN QUESTION"
Originally produced by The WPA Theatre
(Kyle Renick, Artistic Director)
New York City, 1988

"PSYCHO BEACH PARTY"
Presented at The Limbo Lounge
in New York City in October, 1986

Subsequently presented by
Theatre-in-Limbo, Kenneth Elliott and Gerald A. Davis
on July 20, 1987 at the
Players Theatre, New York City

"VAMPIRE LESBIANS OF SODOM" and
"SLEEPING BEAUTY OR COMA"
Presented at The Limbo Lounge
in New York City in 1984

Subsequently presented by
Theatre-in-Limbo, Kenneth Elliott and Gerald A. Davis
on June 19, 1985 at the
Provincetown Playhouse, New York City

THE Lady IN QUESTION?

THE LADY IN QUESTION opened at the Orpheum Theatre in New York City on July 25, 1989. It was directed by Kenneth Elliott. Its setting was designed by B.T. Whitehill, the lighting by Vivien Leone, the costumes by Robert Locke and Jennifer Arnold, the wigs by Elizabeth Katherine Carr. Production Stage Manager was Robert Vandergriff.

The cast was as follows:

Voice of the Announcer	James Cahill
Professor Mittelhoffer	Mark Hamilton
Heidi Mittelhoffer	Theresa Marlowe
Karel Freiser	Robert Carey
Professor Erik Maxwell	Arnie Kolodner
Hugo Hoffmann	Andy Halliday
Baron Wilhelm Von Elsner	Kenneth Elliott
Gertrude Garnet	Charles Busch
Kitty, The Countess de Borgia	Julie Halston
Augusta Von Elsner	Meghan Robinson
Dr. Maximilian	Mark Hamilton
Lotte Von Elsner	Andy Halliday
Raina Aldric	Meghan Robinson

Time: 1940

Place: The Bavarian Alps, outside the train station at Ludwigshafen, and the schloss of the Baron Von Elsner.

*This play is dedicated
with gratitude and deep affection to the
memory of Robert Vandergriff*

AUTHOR'S NOTE

For the past few years, I've been in an incredibly fortunate position. I've had the opportunity to realize many of my more outrageous daydreams. In 1984, Ken Elliott and I started our company, Theatre-in-Limbo. Since then as writer/performer I've been able to go back in time to swinging mod London, ancient Sodom, Malibu Beach circa 1962, and old Spain among others.

In the fall of 1988, we were asked to do a show for the WPA Theatre. I've always had a great fondness for Hollywood anti-Nazi war melodramas of the 1940s. I'm also a delirious fan of the late star, Norma Shearer. The result was "The Lady In Question." So you see, I'm not lampooning these films such as "Escape" or "Above Suspicion" or "Notorious," I'm saluting them. I'm celebrating a time in our country when issues weren't so muddy. There was an indisputable villain and it seemed as if indeed God was on our side.

Therefore, in performing this play, it is important not to "camp" it up and make the characters ridiculous. The style of the piece should be almost exactly the tone of those dark, gray suspense films—only slightly askew. Emotions run a bit too high, tough tootsies are a bit too hardboiled. The audience must not for a moment lose the sense of urgency and pace that all traditional suspense plays should have.

I wrote the role of Gertrude Garnet to be played by myself in drag. I played it very realistically, or rather realistically in the grand manner of the star ladies of the past. I tried to create my own kind of star, but incorporated echoes of Bette Davis, Rosalind Russell, Barbara Stanwyck and of course Norma Shearer.

I see no reason why a woman couldn't play Gertrude Garnet most effectively. I honestly don't think there is a single joke that depends on gender role–reversal. The part of Lotte was also played by a fella, and he doubled as Hugo in the opening of the play. Andy Halliday played Lotte with great integrity and was hysterically funny because he was truly terrifying.

And that really is my point. If you play it right, this is one show where you can have your strudel and eat it too. You can keep the folks laughing and also make them hope you don't get shot in the keyster before the curtain falls.

ACT
ONE

Internationally-renowned concert pianist Gertrude Garnet (Charles Busch) arrives in Ludwigshafen.

Photo by T.L. Boston
Backdrop designed by B.T. Whitehill

PROLOGUE

A large four–paneled screen covers the width of the stage. It is a giant–sized travel folder with the title "Tour Carefree Bavaria." The mood is dark, gray, ominous. Lush movie soundtrack music is heard full of drama and triumph. The music quiets down to a feeling of suspense. A voiceover of a sonorous, old time announcer is heard.

VOICE–OVER: The year is 1940. Adolph Hitler's armies make his dream of European annexation a reality. Norway, the Netherlands, Belgium and France all fall before the monstrous power of the German fighting machine. Fear of fifth columnists makes idle chatter a thing of the past as people across the continent live in terror.

(During the voice–over, KAREL, a handsome, young Nazi stormtrooper goosesteps across the stage and exits)

VOICE–OVER: Nowhere is this more evident than in Hitler's own Bavaria. Free speech and free travel are but a distant memory and those attempting to escape look with sad eyes to their local train terminal as a desperate symbol of hopes and dreams passing by.

(The sounds of a train pulling into the station are heard as the lights come up on Act One, Scene One)

ACT I

Scene One

The train station at Ludwigshafen. Afternoon. PROFESSOR
MITTELHOFFER, *a kindly, mildly eccentric old man awaits the
train from Paris. With him is his daughter* HEIDI. *She is in her
early twenties, very pretty, courageous and something of an
emotional spitfire. Her fragile, Dresden doll appearance belies
her fierce temper.*

PROFESSOR: Heidi, I hope we have not missed his train. You
should have woken me earlier from my snooze.

HEIDI: Papa, don't be silly. We're early. Professor Maxwell is
arriving on the 11:58. And besides, you needed your rest.
You've been slaving over your new translation for weeks.

PROFESSOR: "The Complete Letters of Thomas Jefferson."
How Germany needs his wise words today.

HEIDI: How Germany needs her great men today. True greatness and not this *(with gutteral fierceness)* revolting imitation of . . .

PROFESSOR: Shhhh Heidi! You must control your passionate nature. You inherited that from your mother, may she rest in peace.

HEIDI: Do you miss her terribly?

PROFESSOR: Very much so. *(He sneezes)*

HEIDI: Oh Papa, why are you not wearing your muffler? How many times have I told you?

PROFESSOR: I must have left it where I left my spectacles.

HEIDI *(taking his glasses out of her pocket):* Here are your spectacles. I was wondering when you'd miss them.

PROFESSOR: My little mischief–maker.

HEIDI: What am I to do with you? Sometimes I feel like I am your wife. I like that feeling, Papa. I love you more than anything in the world. I'd kill for you.

PROFESSOR: That is not good, *liebchen.* A young girl must have her own life. I do not want you to develop an Elektra complex.

HEIDI: Papa, I promise you I won't. (KAREL, *a handsome young storm trooper, enters)* Look, Papa, there's Karel.

PROFESSOR: Heidi, don't . . .

HEIDI: Hello, Karel!

(He comes over)

KAREL: Heidi, Professor Mittelhoffer, *heil Hitler.*

PROFESSOR: Good morning, Karel.

KAREL: It is customary in the new order to reply "*Heil Hitler.*"

PROFESSOR: You must forgive me, my lumbago.

HEIDI *(flirtatiously):* Karel, it's been so long since we've . . .

KAREL *(ignoring her):* Professor, what brings you to the terminal so early?

PROFESSOR: I am meeting a colleague.

KAREL: A foreign colleague?

PROFESSOR: As a matter of fact, yes.

KAREL: From what country?

PROFESSOR: I am not aware of his citizenship.

KAREL *(with mounting intensity):* Why does he keep this a secret?

PROFESSOR: I imagine it is his choice.

KAREL: He has no choice. Why is he in Germany?

PROFESSOR: To gaze at our lovely alpine scenery?

KAREL: Do not treat me like a fool. I am no longer your pupil. No more can you make me sit in the corner with a dunce cap. I would not want to report your activities to my superiors.

HEIDI: Karel, you must not speak to my father that way.

KAREL: Your father is a renowned intellectual, a loathsome species, and therefore under suspicion. It is my duty to leave nothing unnoticed.

HEIDI *(flirting):* Then you've been shirking your duties.

KAREL: I have not.

HEIDI: You haven't noticed my pretty new frock.

KAREL: It is most becoming.

PROFESSOR: Excuse us. We must see if the train is late.

HEIDI: Oh, Papa, why don't you check?

PROFESSOR: Heidi, my . . .

HEIDI: Go, go, go.

PROFESSOR: Heidi!

HEIDI: Go.

(The PROFESSOR *exits)*

KAREL: Your father, he does not like me.

HEIDI: No one likes little boys with bad manners.

KAREL: I obey the code of the new order.

HEIDI: Karel, I've missed you.

KAREL: You can see me whenever you choose.

HEIDI: I miss the boy I once loved so dearly. I'm afraid he no longer exists.

KAREL: Heidi, don't.

HEIDI: I miss the boy I tutored every day. Your face was so cute when you'd strain for the simplest answers. For ten points: Name three tragedies by William Shakespeare.

KAREL: Shakespeare is dead. There is only Schiller and Goethe.

HEIDI *(grabbing his head):* Look at me! How do I crack open that big, good–looking, dumb head of yours? How do I let in some truth?

KAREL *(reciting):* Adolf Hitler is our savior. The Third Reich will last a thousand years.

HEIDI *(with wildly fierce emotion):* Shut up and look at me. How do I make you feel, feel something! Anything! For chrissake, be a human being!

KAREL *(breaking into passion):* I am a human being, Heidi, and I do love you, and I'm scared for you. Do not fall back with the malcontents. They will all perish. There is still a place for you in the Hitler Rhinemaiden brigade.

HEIDI: I wouldn't play canasta with those goose–stepping lezzies.

KAREL *(hardened):* I see we are both not the young people we once were.

(PROFESSOR MITTELHOFFER *enters with* PROFESSOR ERIK MAXWELL, *a handsome American. He carries a suitcase)*

PROFESSOR: Heidi, our guest has arrived. We must go.

KAREL: Do not hurry, Professor. I should like to officially greet your esteemed colleague.

PROFESSOR: Professor Maxwell, this is my daughter, Heidi, and my former student, Karel Freiser.

ERIK: I'm flattered that I merit an official greeting.

(Puts down suitcase, stage left)

HEIDI: Your train was exactly on time.

ERIK: Yes, it arrived with frightening German efficiency.

KAREL: You will become accustomed to our well–organized society.

ERIK: It is a lovely country, the land of beer, Wagner and terror.

PROFESSOR *(nervously):* He means terriers, schnauzers, dogs.

KAREL: My English is not fluent. Of course, English is a gutter language, ultimately to be extinguished.

ERIK *(matter of factly):* While it's still spoken, up yours, asshole.

KAREL: I do not comprehend. *Was heisst "asshole"?*

ERIK: It means your Fuhrer.

PROFESSOR: Take my word, Karel, in America, it is used most selectively. Come, you must be hungry.

KAREL: One moment. What is your business here in Germany?

ERIK: It is my business and none of yours, bub.

KAREL: Perhaps it should be the business of the prefect of police. Enjoy your visit, Professor, and let us hope it will be brief. *Heil Hitler.*

(He looks at HEIDI *and exits)*

ERIK: A graduate of Hitler's charm school.

HEIDI: It is foolish to bait him, Professor Maxwell.

ERIK: Forgive me. It was foolish, foolish and selfish. My big mouth will only reflect on you. I'm very sorry.

HEIDI: Your bitterness is understandable.

ERIK: I'm beside myself with worry. Since I received your letter, I haven't slept a wink. How is she? Have you spoken to her? Has there been any word?

PROFESSOR: Yes, there has been word. Can you take it?

ERIK: I can take it.

PROFESSOR: Your mother is to be executed on Friday. (ERIK *starts to swoon, they catch him*) Buck up, my friend.

ERIK *(with rapid-fire delivery):* The monsters! I could kill every one of them with my bare hands. Why should they want her dead? She's an actress. She knows nothing about politics. Dead! That word has nothing to do with my mother. My mother is life, life itself! Why? Why?

PROFESSOR: I have known your mother a great many years. She is a brilliant actress, but "careful" is not a word in her vocabulary. She befriended a young, radical playwright, the hope of the German theatre. *(Embarrassed)* It was rumored they became lovers.

ERIK *(with a deadpan, no-nonsense air):* Professor, let me tell you right now, my parents divorced when I was little. My father was awarded custody and my mother returned to Europe where she has lived her own life. I do not judge her. Please go on with your story.

PROFESSOR: Using her legendary name, they mounted a production of the young man's most fiercely anti–Nazi play. On the opening night, the S.S. raided the theatre, killed the playwright and arrested your mother on the grounds of treason. She is in a prison a few miles away.

ERIK: This is a nightmare!

PROFESSOR: You will wake up, my friend, and soon. We have devised a plan of escape.

ERIK: Escape? Is it possible?

HEIDI: Yes, but exceedingly dangerous.

PROFESSOR: The plan involves the formidable figure of the Baron Von Elsner.

ERIK: Who is this man?

HEIDI: A decadent nobleman who has risen high in the Nazi regime. There are terrible tales of his numerous depravities.

ERIK *(with genuine, high–minded interest):* Spare me nothing.

PROFESSOR: Later, but for our plan to succeed, we need a confederate planted in the Baron's ancestral home. You can see it looming darkly in the mountains.

ERIK: What does the Baron's house have to do with my mother? None of this makes sense.

HEIDI *(urgently):* You must do exactly as my father says.

ERIK: Of course, I trust you both completely. How do I find an ally in the Baron's home?

(HUGO enters. HUGO is an intense, high–strung fellow in his thirties. A touch of Peter Lorre)

PROFESSOR: That I do not know, but the escape must take place tomorrow night.

HEIDI: Papa, there is Hugo Hoffmann.

PROFESSOR: Hoffmann is a noted painter. He has used his gift to forge letters of transit. If we are lucky enough to get your mother out of prison, we will need them to cross the border. He has made four of them. Be careful what you say. There are ears everywhere.

HUGO: Professor, how good to see you. *(Under his breath)* I'm afraid the Baron Von Elsner may be on to my activities. *(Looking at* ERIK*)* Is this the one?

HEIDI: Yes, our friend has many contacts in the theatre and would like to see your sketches.

ERIK *(trembling):* Yes, I'm sure they will travel well in America.

HUGO: Compliment my tie. I will give it to you. Protest, then accept it. The letters of transit are inside the fabric.

ERIK: I do so admire your necktie.

HUGO: Then you must take it as a souvenir of our great country.

ERIK: You are far too generous.

HUGO: No, I insist. *(Takes off his tie and gives it to* ERIK*)*

HEIDI: The Baron.

(The BARON VON ELSNER *enters. The* BARON *is a dignified, imposing man in his forties, a cold–blooded killer but with a silky charm)*

BARON: Could that be the very talented Hugo Hoffmann?

HUGO *(terrified):* Baron, this is an honor.

BARON: I must commend you on the restoration of my frescoes. Most skillful.

(The rest of the scene is underscored by tense, suspenseful music)

HUGO: Thank you, Baron Von Elsner.

BARON: However, your latest creative endeavor disturbs me.

HUGO: The mural at City Hall? It is most reverential.

BARON: You are very clever. It took careful observation, but then I discovered it.

HUGO: I don't know what you mean.

BARON: The magnificent detail surrounding the figure of the Fuhrer is actually a code. A call to arms to your ridiculous resistance movement.

HUGO: That is not true. Perhaps someone has tampered with my painting.

BARON: That could be possible. Come with me to the prefect's office so we can clear up this misconception.

HUGO: By all means. Some traitor has defaced my work. Herr Baron, if I could stop and use the facilities, I'd be most grateful.

BARON: Of course, Hugo, of course.

(HUGO starts to make a run for it. KAREL enters to block his way. HUGO turns to the PROFESSOR)

HUGO: Help me, help me, please.

PROFESSOR: What can I do?

(HUGO *jumps off the front of the stage and makes a run for it*)

BARON: Halt! Halt in the name of the Fuhrer!

(BARON *shoots* HUGO *in the back.* HUGO *falls down, dead, beyond the view of the audience.* HEIDI *screams. The* BARON *and* KAREL *exit.* ERIK, *the* PROFESSOR *and* HEIDI *are horror–struck and hurry away.* ERIK *leaves his suitcase stage left. The lights dim)*

VOICE–OVER: Yes, human life is cheap in the fatherland. The time has come for all men to come to the aid of humanity, to cast off self–interest and band together. But, as always, there are SOME PEOPLE who ignore the cataclysm around them. SOME PEOPLE who live only for their hedonistic pleasure. SOME PEOPLE WHO DON'T GIVE A GOOD GODDAM FOR ANYONE BUT THEIR OWN STINKIN' SELVES!

(The glamourous, internationally acclaimed American concert pianist, GERTRUDE GARNET *[pronounced* GAR–NAY*] enters, having just arrived on the Paris train. She's elegantly dressed in a traveling suit and furs. She speaks in a grand, very affected manner that disguises her honky–tonk background. At this moment, she's in a terrible snit)*

GERTRUDE: Where is she? Where is my maid? Suzette! Suzette! If that dreadful girl thinks she can leave me high and dry without my cosmetic bag, she's got another think coming. *(Looks around)* Conductor! Conductor! Where is everyone? Kitty! Kitty!

(KITTY, THE COUNTESS DE BORGIA, *enters.* KITTY *is* GERTRUDE'*s longtime buddy from her vaudeville days.* KITTY *is an attractive blonde, wisecracking, tough as nails but with a heart of gold. Now married to a nobleman,* KITTY *too can affect a high tone when it's required)*

KITTY: Hold your horses, Gertie. These gams are still moving on Palm Beach time.

GERTRUDE: This is absolutely appalling. How could Suzette do this to me? Quitting without even giving notice.

KITTY: You shouldn't have slapped her across the face with that paillard of veal.

GERTRUDE: I was making a point.

KITTY: You sure made it. The dame jumped off a moving train.

GERTRUDE: I never dreamed she'd be so vindictive. Fleeing with my cosmetic bag. The lashes alone are worth over a thousand dollars. Why are there so many soldiers about with their great scowling faces?

KITTY: Honey, I say we get back on that train and skip this part of the tour.

GERTRUDE *(aghast):* Skip this part of the tour? Kitty, my recitals in Munich, Frankfurt, and Ludwigshafen were scheduled four years ago and are completely sold out.

KITTY: Give 'em back their money and let's beat it. This whole country gives me the creeps.

GERTRUDE: Kitty, I am an artist, the leading concert pianist on the international stage, and when Gertrude Garnet says she'll appear, she appears, hands oiled and ready. Where is the car from the hotel?

KITTY *(laughs):* You know, Gertie, this reminds me of our old vaudeville days when we were left stranded in Altoona.

GERTRUDE: Kitty, this is hardly the time.

KITTY: We were booked on the same bill as that slimy escape artist.

GERTRUDE: He was a mentalist. Is that the car?

KITTY: Whatever, he escaped with the cashbox.

GERTRUDE: And because you gave him the romantic fisheye, the manager thought we was in cahoots.

KITTY: I never gave him the fisheye.

GERTRUDE: Ahh, you were dropping them eyelids like they were a fire-curtain. And that stingy manager, he was as tight as Kelsey's nuts. *(Regains her soignée tone)* Kitty, I am not in the mood for strolling down memory lane.

KITTY: Well, you should. You've become just too hoity-toity since you took up that egghead music.

GERTRUDE: That egghead music has paid off in spades.

KITTY: I still say you were a lot happier when we were in vaudeville and I played fiddle to your honky-tonk piana.

GERTRUDE: Now you're a wealthy Countess, I hardly see you renewing your union cards.

KITTY: Sister, after having the Count de Borgia rubbing his old sausage on me, gimme a split week in Pittsburgh.

GERTRUDE: Stop that. We've risen to the top of high society and do you know how we made it?

KITTY: Behind a lot of wives' backs.

GERTRUDE: No, because it was our destiny. I've been seeing the most marvelous mystic, so wise, and terribly profound.

KITTY: Not another one. That last holy man gave me one helluva goose.

GERTRUDE: Not the swami. He's laid out for me the entire blueprint of life. He calls it his New World Philosophy. Everything that happens to us happens because we make it happen. There was no luck involved in my career. *(With a rather frightening hard edge)* I made my luck.

KITTY: So you mean somehow we wanted to be stranded in this train station?

GERTRUDE: Indeed. Perhaps instinctively we know that some great adventure lies in store for us. You see, darling, the rhythms and patterns of millions of years of civilization have brought you and me to this very moment. Now it remains for us to choose how we're going to handle this occasion. We *can* change the pattern.

KITTY *(not impressed):* Change the tune, girl, the record's got a scratch on it.

GERTRUDE: Stop that, Kitty, this is important.

KITTY: I just have trouble believing that if our train had crashed, it would have been because I chose it.

(ERIK *enters and as he passes the ladies on his way to get his suitcase, he can't help hearing what they are saying)*

GERTRUDE: Entirely possible. Sometimes I think all these people who say they're being persecuted, perhaps they chose it too. Unconsciously, of course. It does make it rather hard to sympathize though, doesn't it?

ERIK: That is the stupidest hogwash I've ever heard.

GERTRUDE *(haughtily):* I beg your pardon??!!

ERIK: That half–baked philosophy is extremely dangerous.

GERTRUDE *(aside to* KITTY*):* Kitty, he's a nut, move over.

(GERTRUDE *pulls* KITTY *over a bit stage right)*

ERIK: Open your eyes, lady. Innocent people are disappearing around you. The Nazis are planning to tattoo people to sepa-rate them from the rest of us. There are stories of hideous camps built to isolate those out of political favor.

GERTRUDE *(blithely):* Such an alarmist. Besides, we all have many reincarnations. This one may be dreary, chances are the next one will be all champagne and caviar.

ERIK: One day, you're going to be shaken out of this foolish-ness and I'll feel very sorry for you.

GERTRUDE: Sing no sad songs for me, darling. Come, Kitty.

ERIK: You're famous, aren't you?

GERTRUDE: Extremely famous and extremely bored.

ERIK: You're Gertrude Garnet. *(Pronounces her name like the birthstone)*

GERTRUDE *(irritated):* Gertrude Garnet. [Garnay]

KITTY: You're an American. Are you here for work or amuse-ment?

GERTRUDE: Kitty.

ERIK: I have important work in Germany.

KITTY: I hope it won't take up all of your time.

GERTRUDE *(to herself):* I can't believe I'm waiting out here without a car.

ERIK: Where are you staying?

GERTRUDE:	KITTY:	ERIK:
We're staying with friends.	The Hotel . . .	I don't mean to pry.
	That's not true.	I thought perhaps we . . .

Kitty, don't . . .   The Hotel Mitzi.

ERIK: The Hotel Mitzi. I read about that in the newspaper. Yes, it was confiscated last week. When the concierge protested, he and his entire staff were executed.

KITTY: How dreadful.

GERTRUDE: Dreadful indeed. It's Oktoberfest and we'll never find another reservation.

(The BARON *enters)*

KITTY: What are we going to do?

*(*GERTRUDE *approaches the* BARON *and asks him, in German, where she can find a hotel)*

GERTRUDE: *Mein herr, mein herr, entshuldigen Sie bitte, mein herr. Meine freundin und ich suchen Unterkunft.*

BARON: I speak English, Madame Garnet.

GERTRUDE *(pleased):* Oh.

BARON: I would recognize you anywhere. I am the Baron Von Elsner.

(Attempting to take her hand, she withdrawing it)

GERTRUDE *(laughing):* I'm afraid I never let anyone touch my hands. They're insured by Lloyds of London.

BARON *(with great charm):* I can well understand. I have many of your recordings in my home. Your boxed set of Schubert is a particular favorite.

GERTRUDE: The German composers are so good for the fingers. Have you heard my Beethoven "Appassionata"?

BARON: It haunts me. I'm particularly fond of your Schumann "Fantasy Stucke."

GERTRUDE: Oh, and this is my traveling companion, the Countess de Borgia.

BARON *(taking her hand):* And are your hands insured?

KITTY *(coldly):* Just personal liability.

BARON *(to* GERTRUDE *with veiled irony):* Your friend is very amusing. *(To* KITTY*)* You must visit our local circus. Unfortunately, our leading clown was mauled to death by an angry lion. I have not been introduced to your other friend.

GERTRUDE: We just met him.

ERIK: Professor Erik Maxwell.

BARON: And your field of expertise?

ERIK: Nutrition. I'm making a study of German dietary habits.

BARON: Yes?

ERIK: I believe there is a connection between the heartiness of German beer and bread and your legendary ambition.

BARON: We do eat very well, but you must not forget, we are the master race. Now, my dear Madame Garnet, you were asking me something.

GERTRUDE: The Countess and I are in terrible straits. We had reservations at the Hotel Mitzi, and now I hear it's closed. Could you recommend some first–class hostelry?

BARON: The Mitzi was a dreadful place. May I offer you the use of my schloss?

KITTY: Come again.

GERTRUDE: His schloss, dear, his villa. We couldn't possibly accept.

BARON: It is quite lovely, right on the lake at Shauffehausen.

KITTY: I've never been inside a real German slush.

GERTRUDE: Schloss, dear. Perhaps we could spend the night, until we find further accommodations.

BARON: Delighted. Professor Maxwell, you must join us for dinner. I find your theories most intriguing.

ERIK: I will be there. Goodbye, ladies.

KITTY: Then we'll see you later at the Baron's schnapps.

GERTRUDE: Schloss, dear.

KITTY: Right.

ERIK: Till then.

(He exits)

BARON: Shall we go? I'll have my manservant collect your luggage.

GERTRUDE: Just those thirty–seven pieces. This is such a lovely surprise. Baron, I simply can't wait to see your magnificent shlong. I mean, schloss!

(They all exit. Blackout. Wagner's "Liebestod" is heard in Liszt's piano transcription. As the action moves into the next scene that evening, the music becomes GERTRUDE's *playing in the adjoining salon.)*

ACT I

Scene Two

The schloss of the BARON VON ELSNER, *that evening. The ski lodge has been the* VON ELSNER's *vacation home for generations and reflects their malevolence in its cold, gray austerity. A grotesque boar's head is their notion of whimsical decor. There is a front door u.s.c. and a fireplace d.s.l. Above the fireplace is a portrait of Hitler. A large sofa center stage is the only furniture. A staircase starts u.s.r. and goes to a landing above the front door. There are two doors on this landing. Downstairs s.r. there are two doors: One to the kitchen (large swinging door) and d.s. of that door is the door to the concert room. On s.l. above the fireplace an archway leads to the library. We hear* GERTRUDE *playing the piano in the concert salon.* KAREL *enters the front door with the very elegant* BARONESS AUGUSTA VON ELSNER. *White–haired and magnificent, she is the* BARON's *mother. Her aristocratic charm masks an evil, cold spirit.*

AUGUSTA: Ah, how grand to be home. Thank you, Karel, for escorting me from the train.

KAREL: It is my honor, Baroness.

AUGUSTA *(with grandeur):* This solid entry bids me welcome and gives me strength. Indeed, no one would dare invade my portal. My, what lovely playing. Is that a new recording?

KAREL: The Baron is giving a party and the American pianist, Gertrude Garnet, is the guest of honor.

AUGUSTA *(somewhat disturbed):* An American? How very interesting.

(The BARON *enters from the salon)*

BARON: Mother, you've arrived, looking splendid. We've missed you.

(The BARON *removes her cape)*

AUGUSTA: I arrive home a day early and a grand soirée is in progress.

BARON *(giving cape to* KAREL*):* An intimate supper party, nothing more. Karel, you may go.

KAREL: Yes, your excellency. *(Hangs cape in closet next to front door and exits)*

BARON: Now Mother, tell me of your visit to Heidelberg.

AUGUSTA: Who is this American piano player?

BARON: Gertrude Garnet is a world famous artist. She is to perform at the *Festspielhaus* next Tuesday. Madame Garnet and her friend, the Countess de Borgia, will be staying with us.

AUGUSTA: The Countess, an Italian?

BARON: No, she too is an American.

AUGUSTA *(thinking it over):* Two Americans under our roof?

BARON: Yes, and they are charming ladies. Come Mother, you must hear Madame Garnet play.

AUGUSTA: Two Americans under our roof? Willy, is this prudent?

BARON: I see no reason why it should not be.

AUGUSTA: My dear son, we shall be at war with their country at any moment. What could you be thinking of? I am astonished. The Fuhrer will not find this to his liking.

BARON *(exploding):* Mother, I will not be bullied by you or the Fuhrer, do you hear me? *(Stamps his foot)*

AUGUSTA: Wilhelm!!! Don't you dare raise your voice to me, not in my house!

BARON *(meekly):* Forgive me, Mother.

AUGUSTA: After you have finished entertaining these creatures, you will find them accommodations in the village for the night.

BARON *(quietly):* Mother, that I cannot do.

AUGUSTA: Willy, is there something you're not telling me? What is it? You and I have no secrets. We are partners, soldiers in arms.

BARON: Madame Garnet . . . I am in love with her.

AUGUSTA: Willy.

BARON: I have met her but this morning and I am passionately in love.

AUGUSTA: You cut a ludicrous figure. You are not a schoolboy with an idiotic infatuation. You are a commanding officer, serving the greatest leader in the history of the world. Now straighten your back and remember your duties. I shall telephone the inn and find these women lodging.

(She picks up the telephone on the mantle. The BARON *stops her)*

BARON: You don't seem to understand, Mother. I plan to marry her. She shall be the next Baroness Von Elsner.

AUGUSTA *(putting down the phone receiver, with great intensity):* Wilhelm, if you persist in this foolishness, before all the servants . . .

BARON: I do not wish to argue. Have you never fallen in love at first sight? Of course you have, my darling, beautiful Maman. Surely with Father.

AUGUSTA: Indeed not. The marriage was contracted at birth. You should know. For centuries the Von Elsners have married their first cousins.

(The music ends, we hear applause)

BARON: Please, Mother, do not be rude to her.

AUGUSTA: I am never rude.

*(*GERTRUDE *enters in a magnificent evening gown. She is followed by* KITTY, ERIK *and* DR. MAXIMILIAN. *The* DOKTOR *is an elegant Nazi aristocrat in his forties. He,* KITTY *and* ERIK *carry drinks)*

DOKTOR: Brilliant, simply brilliant, so passionate and yet so effortless.

GERTRUDE: That is, of course, the secret to playing Wagner. One must and I say, one must, read his score as one would read Shakespeare. The notes themselves always dictate the emotion. *(To* AUGUSTA*)* Dear, I left my drink on the piano. *(To the* DOKTOR*)* When I first approach any score, I look . . .

BARON: Madame Garnet, this is my mother, the Baroness Von Elsner.

DOKTOR: Augusta, we did not expect you until tomorrow.

AUGUSTA: Evidently, Doktor Maximilian. I see you have taken time off from your medical experiments.

DOKTOR: It has been well worth it. I only wish you had arrived earlier to partake of Madame Garnet's genius.

AUGUSTA: I am sure we will hear more from Fraulein Garnet before her visit is over.

BARON *(with a note of warning): Mutter, Du hast versprochen. Dich gut zu benehmen.* [Mother, you promised you would behave.]

AUGUSTA *(disgusted): Was siehst Du in Ihr? Sie ist so vulgaer and buergerlich.* [What do you see in her? She is so vulgar and common.]

BARON: *Mutter, beleidige Sie nicht. Ich warne Dich.* [Mother, do not embarrass her. I'm warning you.]

AUGUSTA: *Drohe Deiner Mutter nicht.* [Do not threaten me.]

GERTRUDE *(oblivious):* Love your hair. What would you call that color?

KITTY: Battleship gray.

BARON: Mother, the Countess de Borgia and Professor Maxwell.

ERIK: A pleasure.

AUGUSTA: Another American. *Ach du leiber.* Has our country been invaded in my absence?

BARON: Mother is quite comical. You know the German sense of humor.

(GERTRUDE *laughs gaily, then abruptly stops when she realizes there was nothing funny*)

AUGUSTA: Madame Garnet, forgive my ignorance of your remarkable career. As chairwoman of the Reich Committee for the Preservation of the Teutonic Arts, I have devoted myself to the work of exclusively German artists. Do you include any Strauss in your repertoire?

GERTRUDE *(with charm):* Indeed. His "Bein Schlafengehen" is a concert staple of mine.

AUGUSTA *(appalled):* An American playing "Bein Schlafengehen." No doubt you also perform his "Burlesque in D."

GERTRUDE *(understands the bitchiness behind the remark):* I sure do. I'm also quite adept with Liszt, particularly his "Weiner, Klager, Sorgan, Zagen."

AUGUSTA *(topping her in bitchiness):* Really, of course, a true test would be Schumann's "Warter, Warter, Wilder, Schiffsmann."

GERTRUDE *(the war escalates):* I play it with my eyes closed. Honey, get me in the right mood, and I'll hit you with my "Faschingsschwank aus Wein"!

AUGUSTA: I am sure you do quite a raucous "Freulings Fahrt"!!

GERTRUDE *(mad):* Oh yeah!

(LOTTE, *the* BARON*'s teenage niece, appears at the top of the stairs. With blond braids, elaborate traditional German costume, she is a twelve year old demon)*

LOTTE *(scampering down the stairs):* Uncle, Uncle, why did the pretty music stop?

BARON: Lotte, what are you doing up so late?

LOTTE: Uncle Willy, I heard the music. It was ever so lovely.

BARON: Madame Garnet, my niece Lotte.

GERTRUDE: Perfectly charming.

AUGUSTA: Madame Garnet and her friends are from America.

LOTTE: America. That dreadful place, so dirty, so crowded. All the races mixed up. *(To* KITTY*)* You have such a funny face. Doesn't she have a funny face? You must be a combination of a million races.

KITTY: I sure am, honey, but you're pure bitch.

GERTRUDE: Kitty, that's a terrible thing to say.

KITTY: It must be this German firewater. I apologize, dear.

AUGUSTA: You will find Lotte quite precocious. She has a great interest in history.

DOKTOR: She knows far more than I do.

LOTTE *(with perverse enthusiasm):* Oh yes, I practically live at the prison museum. Do you know they have a complete fourteenth–century dungeon. They have a rare torture device whereupon four prongs are attached to the prisoner's face and then stretched in four different directions.

KITTY: A totalitarian face–lift.

BARON: Shall we have coffee in the library? Cook brews an excellent café Viennese, and we will have some chocolates.

LOTTE: May I come, Uncle? I love sweets.

BARON: May she, Mother?

AUGUSTA: All right, but do not overindulge. Chocolate gives you acne.

(She exits, MAXIMILIAN *follows)*

KITTY *(to* LOTTE): Oh, don't worry, honey, tomorrow we'll find you a nice medieval pimple popper.

(She exits, followed by LOTTE, *then* ERIK. *The* BARON *stops* GERTRUDE)

BARON: Gertrude, this has been such a delightful surprise, meeting you.

GERTRUDE: And you were a godsend. I really don't know what we would have done.

BARON: I only wish I could spend more time with you. I have so many meetings and military obligations. I hope you won't find our little village too tiresome.

GERTRUDE: Oh no, I adore *quiet* places.

BARON: Away from the glamour of Manhattan?

GERTRUDE: Rather.

BARON: Away from the many stage door Johnnies. Isn't that what you call them?

GERTRUDE *(amused):* Yes, that's what we call them.

BARON: I imagine a woman of your fame and beauty has many, how do I say, flirtations?

GERTRUDE: Fewer than you may think. I'm completely devoted to two figures, the bass and treble clefts. *(She sits on sofa)*

BARON: Is there no place in your life for love? *(He sits beside her)*

GERTRUDE: I'm not too keen on love, never having known it. Besides, my spiritual adviser, the swami, had made me realize that I can't love others until I love myself first. I must be number one. And I can only make others happy after I have made myself completely happy, first and foremost. It may take years.

BARON: You're very mysterious, Gertrude. As mysterious as a prelude by Debussy.

GERTRUDE: Am I? *(She plays piano scales on her arm of the sofa)*

BARON: Such beautiful hands. Let me see them. Ah, lovely. So delicate. *(She displays her hands in a picturesque manner)*

GERTRUDE: Yes. Every finger is double–jointed and X–rays have revealed large air pockets in the bone marrow.

BARON: So sensitive and yet so practical. Rather like myself. I feel as if we were two melodies that fit together in perfect counterpoint.

GERTRUDE: I'm flattered, your excellency.

BARON: Your excellency? Why so formal? You Americans are so famous for your nicknames. What shall you call me?

GERTRUDE *(flirtatiously):* Well, for Wilhelm, I could call you "Bill." And, of course, you are a bit older than I. I could call you "Popsie."

BARON *(laughs):* No, I don't care for that. What about "darling"?

GERTRUDE: Don't you think that's a bit too intimate?

BARON *(intimately, as he rises):* No, I don't. And to demonstrate our intimacy, I shall let you in on a little secret. I'm going to show you something of mine I don't let everyone see.

GERTRUDE *(dubious):* Oh, yeah?

BARON: You see that portrait of the Fuhrer?

GERTRUDE: An excellent likeness.

BARON *(pulling it away, revealing a safe):* It conceals a safe. Most clever. Everything of importance is locked in that safe. Let me see if I can remember the combination. Now, close your eyes. *(She does. He murmurs the combinations, she mouths it to remember)* Turn right three times to zero, left all the way round to six, right back to twelve. Open Sesame. Voila!

GERTRUDE *(standing and crossing to BARON):* Whatcha got in there, Billy boy?

BARON: All sorts of goodies. This ring once belonged to the Grand–duchess Mathilde.

GERTRUDE: Ooh, Daddy, emeralds. *(He gives her the ring)*

BARON: It looks lovely with your hair. Try it on. *(She puts on the ring)* Most attractive. It's yours.

GERTRUDE: I couldn't possibly . . .

BARON: Please, it gives me pleasure, but for now, when you see Mother, turn the ring around.

GERTRUDE: By all means.

BARON *(being silly):* And there's more where that comes from, baby. But only for the girl that I marry.

GERTRUDE: Mmmm, you're tempting me. And all in that safe?

BARON: No, no, no, no. They are in a special vault. The most precious object in this safe is this set of keys. The keys to every room in the house and for the rooms off the catacomb.

GERTRUDE: The catacomb?

BARON: The house was built in the fifteenth century. My warrior ancestors built a mile–long network of tunnels leading away from the house as an escape route.

GERTRUDE: And where does it end?

BARON: A nasty place. Let's not speak of it, particularly when these keys lead to such nice places, such as the vault where we keep the family jewels. *(He returns the keys and locks the safe)* Now, my darling, does that illustrate our intimacy and my trust?

(ERIK *enters*)

GERTRUDE: I promise I won't betray it.

BARON: Ah, Professor Maxwell, do come in.

ERIK: I don't wish to intrude.

BARON: You did, but you are forgiven. Gertrude, I must check on Mother. She was away for the weekend and I haven't even asked about her trip. She can be a real Tartar when she feels ignored. Will you miss me?

GERTRUDE: Unendurably.

BARON: My darling. *(He exits)*

ERIK: You two get along very well.

GERTRUDE: He's sweet.

ERIK: Like a tarantula.

GERTRUDE *(as a warning):* He is our host.

ERIK: I must apologize for my rudeness this morning. I was a busybody and deserved the treatment I got.

GERTRUDE: I too was at fault. But with my maid running off and the loss of our hotel reservation, I really was at sixes and sevens.

ERIK: Then, friends?

GERTRUDE: Friends.

ERIK: It sure is good hearing an American voice. I like talking to you, even beefing with you.

GERTRUDE: A good fight does wonders for the circulation.

ERIK: Then I must be in excellent health. I'm afraid I'm not adjusting very well to the German way.

GERTRUDE: Really, I wonder why. It couldn't be more lovely. And the people are so warm, so friendly, so, how do you they say it, *gemutlich.*

ERIK: Haven't you noticed the fear in everyone's eyes?

GERTRUDE: Fear? What are they afraid of?

ERIK: Miss Garnet, surely you read the newspapers. Germany is in the grip of an evil dictator. The whole country's gone mad. Such arrogance. I tell you, I've had it up to here.

(He raises his arm in a "Heil Hitler" salute)

GERTRUDE: I never, never discuss politics. I am an artist, the world is my stage. Now what else can I do for you?

ERIK: I can't help feeling we've met before.

GERTRUDE: When you're a great celebrity, you find this happens quite often.

ERIK: It was on the stage, but not in a concert hall. Where could it have been? My God, it was in a beer hall . . .

GERTRUDE *(with forced gaiety):* A beer hall?

ERIK: . . . a beer hall in . . . Sandusky, Ohio . . .

GERTRUDE: I hardly think . . .

ERIK: . . . nearly fifteen years ago. You weren't wearing much either . . .

GERTRUDE *(indignant):* Now really . . .

ERIK: Now I remember, didn't you used to be Barrelhouse Gertie, the Kissing Kitten on the Keys?

GERTRUDE *(with vulgar roughness):* Oh, shut up.

ERIK: Then I am correct?

GERTRUDE *(tough and common):* So what of it. I never said I was an overnight success. Okay, Charlie Chan, what's your angle?

ERIK: I'm hoping to find underneath your glamourous facade, the real woman.

GERTRUDE: What for?

ERIK: Because I must ask her a deep favor.

GERTRUDE *(irritated):* Now it comes. How much do you want?

ERIK: I don't ask this favor for myself, but for someone I love very much: my mother. It's dangerous for me to speak to you here.

GERTRUDE: Spill it now.

ERIK: My mother, my mother is also a great artist, an actress, her name is Raina Aldric.

GERTRUDE *(impressed):* Raina Aldric is your mother? I saw her on the stage when I was very young, a great actress. How can I be of any help to her?

ERIK *(bitterly):* As we speak, she lies dying in a Nazi prison only a mile away.

GERTRUDE: A prison so near by?

ERIK: A prison for political prisoners. My mother was arrested for appearing in a play that dared speak against the new order. For this hideous crime, she is sentenced to death.

GERTRUDE: That poor woman.

ERIK: But in a mad world, sometimes one can succeed with a mad act.

GERTRUDE *(nervously):* What are you saying?

ERIK: I have friends here, brave, wonderful people who have planned her escape tomorrow. I can't tell you the details now, but there is one fatally missing link. We need an ally here in the Baron's home.

GERTRUDE *(breaking away from him):* You mustn't ask me this.

ERIK: I beg you, please help me.

GERTRUDE: I dare not.

ERIK: Please. Please.

GERTRUDE *(frightened):* I'm a simple, ordinary woman, extraordinarily talented perhaps but in every other way, ordinary. I am not capable of such heroism.

ERIK: Then you're a coward, a selfish, egocentric, opportunistic, vulgar, manipulating cunt!

GERTRUDE: Vulgar! Now that did it. Look here, you. I don't owe you or your old lady anything. I pay my own freight, never asking for a handout. Now, you must excuse me. I must join my host, the Sacher torte is said to be divine.

ERIK: Yes, gobble down their Nazi food, guzzle their Nazi wine, and try to sleep tonight.

GERTRUDE: You go too far.

ERIK *(grabbing her):* Please help me, I don't even know what I'm saying anymore. I'm desperate. You are our only hope. If you don't help us, Raina Aldric will die on Friday. Please, please help me!

(She breaks away from his grasp as the BARON *enters)*

BARON: I seem to be interrupting a passionate scene.

ERIK: I was demonstrating a new method to save someone from choking.

BARON: She will have no need of that. I hope you have enjoyed yourself, Professor Maxwell. I have done my best to be hospitable. Food and intelligent conversation, my favorite pastimes.

ERIK: And at times, equally hard to swallow.

BARON: Not in my house. We all tend to think the right ideas.

ERIK: Or rather, forced to think the right ideas.

GERTRUDE *(alarmed):* Erik!

BARON *(intrigued):* Erik? You have become quite intimate.

(A Strauss waltz is heard in the salon)

BARON: Professor, I don't think I like you. I shall remember this evening. *(To* GERTRUDE*)* My darling, they are playing a Strauss waltz. Will you indulge me in a spin, if my impudent friend will permit?

(Terribly torn, GERTRUDE *looks first at* ERIK, *then at the* BARON. *They form a triangle. She makes her choice and crosses vivaciously to the* BARON*)*

GERTRUDE: But of course. A waltz can be marvelously divert-
ing.

(The music swells, the BARON *leads* GERTRUDE *in a waltz. He moves her in a circle, but as she spins around to face the audience, the look on her face is one of agonized guilt. Lights fade to black.)*

ACT I

Scene Three

The music fades out. Lights up and we are in the catacomb below the schloss. It is morning. A backdrop is in that shows the catacomb in its creepy, black, dank state. HEIDI is garbed as a prison guard. With her in a wheelchair is the legendary RAINA ALDRIC. RAINA is a beautiful woman in her fifties, fragile but still dramatically vibrant. She lives on drama and speaks in the manner of a wildly flamboyant stage actress.

HEIDI: That was close. I was sure the guard saw through my disguise. You may rest now, Madame Aldric. For the moment, you are safe.

RAINA: Safe. The most beautiful word in any language. But where am I? What time of day is it? I'm so bewildered.

HEIDI: You poor darling. It's early morning. A short while ago, I moved you out of the prison infirmary, took you through the secret door and we came down that very long tunnel. We are now in a room off that tunnel and directly underneath the home of the Baron Von Elsner.

RAINA: A baronial home. I do not understand.

HEIDI: The Baron's ancestors built two fortresses, one they lived in and the other was a prison. They linked them together with a long series of catacombs in case of enemy attack. That door leads to the interior of the Baron's home and to freedom.

RAINA: Why are we waiting? We should go through it now.

HEIDI: The door is locked from the outside. We must wait till my father or Erik opens it and escorts us through the house late tonight.

RAINA (*with great theatricality*): Freedom! I shall never be free. I have seen too much and I shall never be free of the memories. They have destroyed me. I no longer even have the will to walk.

HEIDI: You are a great actress. You have so much more to give.

RAINA: I was once a great actress. "The shining beacon of the European stage" was what Brecht once called me. "Aldric's Hilde Wangel sang with a poetry Ibsen could only hint at," *Munich Bugle*, September 9, 1934. "Raina Aldric's Ranyefskaya ranks with the Cathedral of Chartres as one of the world's great artistic treasures," *Lisbon Daily News*, May 12, 1937. But now I'm old, weak, my legs are worn–out pipe cleaners. You should have let them execute me. My soul died the night they shot my lover, Gebhardt. "Don't shoot him, don't, don't shoot!" Bang, bang, bang. "Then kill me too, kill me!" (HEIDI *bursts into tears*) Forgive me, I didn't mean to upset you.

HEIDI: No, it's just that I too was once in love.

RAINA: Is he dead?

HEIDI: He might as well be. His name was Karel, the most wonderful boy in the world. It seems a century ago that we lay in the *weinerwald* and he taught me the names of all the birds and flowers that gathered about us.

RAINA: What happened?

HEIDI: He came under the influence of the Baron Von Elsner. They have turned his brains to *sauerkraut*. When I look into his beautiful eyes, I only see swastikas. *(Weeping vulnerably)* Madame Aldric, tell me, help me understand why he has turned against me. *(With fierce, hardened vengeance)* Oh, God, how I hate them. They've made this whole goddam world LOUSY! Well, something has changed in Heidi Mittelhoffer and I'm gonna make those bastards pay for what they've done. They've butchered my dreams!!!!

(KITTY *and* GERTRUDE, *laughing, are heard offstage, unlocking the door*)

GERTRUDE *(offstage):* Kitty, this has got to be the right key.

KITTY *(offstage):* Gertie, give it a break.

GERTRUDE *(offstage):* I wanna see those family jewels if it's the last thing I do. I didn't open that damn safe for nix. *(She opens the door)*

HEIDI: Someone's coming.

KITTY: I gotta sit down. This tunnel is as long as Gary Cooper's . . . *(They see* RAINA *and* HEIDI*)* Oh, I'm so sorry.

GERTRUDE: We're guests of the Baron. We were having a marvelous time exploring his lovely home.

KITTY: We didn't mean to intrude.

GERTRUDE *(to* HEIDI*):* You were at the train yesterday, weren't you?

HEIDI: Yes, I was meeting my father.

KITTY: Your friend looks ill.

HEIDI: No, she's quite all right.

KITTY: She's pale as a ghost and trembling. She should see a doctor.

RAINA: Thank you for your concern. I'm recovering from an illness.

KITTY: Your voice is so familiar. Are you an actress?

RAINA: Oh no, never.

KITTY: Of course you are. Why, you're Raina Aldric.

GERTRUDE *(shocked):* Raina Aldric. But I thought you were . . .

HEIDI: Please, please, you must pretend you've never seen us.

KITTY: What do you mean?

GERTRUDE: Kitty, we should leave this place and do as she says.

KITTY: Are you a guest of the Baron's? But why are you in this drafty, cold room? Come, we'll take you upstairs where it's warm.

HEIDI: No, you mustn't.

RAINA: Please, I am quite all right. *(She has a sudden attack of pain in her heart)* A toothache.

KITTY: This is silly, you must come with us.

GERTRUDE: Kitty, Madame Aldric is a prisoner of the Nazis. I believe this young woman has engineered her escape.

KITTY: This is utterly mad. How do you know of this?

GERTRUDE: Erik Maxwell told me and he . . . he is her son.

RAINA: Erik, you know my Erik?

GERTRUDE: Yes, I do.

RAINA: You must be the one. The ruby red hair. A gift from heaven.

GERTRUDE: It's actually a gift of henna.

RAINA: You are the one in my dream. I have a recurring dream that my Erik is walking through the snow with a beautiful young woman with long red hair. I know in my heart, she is the woman he shall marry.

GERTRUDE: I hardly know him.

RAINA: I feel it in my heart. *(She has another heart attack)*

GERTRUDE: He's really quite a guy. Come, Kitty, we should return before our absence draws attention.

KITTY: Was Erik enlisting your help? He was, wasn't he?

GERTRUDE: Yes, he was.

KITTY *(very gung-ho):* Why didn't you tell me? What do we do? How do we proceed?

HEIDI: You must forgive me. I didn't know you had agreed to help.

RAINA: You are both most courageous.

KITTY: Forget that. Just fill me in.

HEIDI: This morning, disguised as a guard, I moved Madame Aldric out of the prison, through the tunnel and into this room under the Baron's shloss.

GERTRUDE *(it all dawns on her):* Yes, of course.

HEIDI: We are to remain here for eighteen hours, at which time, one of you will unlock this room and usher us through the house.

KITTY: Yes, and then?

HEIDI: At precisely midnight, a car will be waiting at the servants' entrance to drive us to the airfield and a plane which will fly us to Switzerland.

KITTY: Well, count me in.

GERTRUDE: Kitty, we must talk. You will excuse us.

KITTY: Let's run upstairs, and rustle up some blankets, hot coffee and crullers. Then we can . . .

GERTRUDE: Kitty, stop it.

KITTY: Gertie, what's wrong?

GERTRUDE: Nothing.

KITTY *(the light beginning to dawn on her):* Gertie, I don't know, but I'm beginning to believe you refused Erik. You refused to help his mother. Tell me I'm wrong.

GERTRUDE *(to* RAINA): We'll get you some crullers . . .

KITTY: You did refuse him, didn't you?

GERTRUDE: Please, Kitty, let's go upstairs.

KITTY: No, answer me. I want the truth.

GERTRUDE: Yes, I refused him. I'd botch it up. I'd be a hindrance.

KITTY *(quietly):* That's not the reason, and you know it. *(Painfully)* You're selfish, Gertie. All your life you've thought of no one but yourself.

GERTRUDE: This is hardly the time for a character analysis.

(GERTRUDE *turns away from* KITTY, *her face obscured*)

KITTY: I'm seeing you as if for the very first time. Oh, Gertie, your face has a terrible look to it.

(GERTRUDE *turns around. Her face looks like a grotesque version of Ma Barker. She realizes this and tries to restrain it*) Go ahead. I'm going to stay.

GERTRUDE: Kitty, you fool, this is serious business. This isn't some madcap caper with your Palm Beach eccentrics. If the Nazis catch you aiding the escape of a prisoner, you'd be lucky merely to be shot.

KITTY: We just won't fail. Besides, I'm not a citizen of Germany.

GERTRUDE: No, but all your finances are tied up in Italy. I've read enough to know that Germany and Italy are allies. You could lose your entire fortune.

KITTY: Sister, with this face, I'll never starve. Now, are you going to help?

GERTRUDE: No, I can't. Nothing personal, Madame Aldric, but I'm scared. Scared to death. I'm not courageous. I like a warm, comfortable bed, a fur coat, dinner and dancing at the Stork Club. I'm not cut out for self–sacrifice. I'm leaving. I must put in my three hours' daily practice, I have a concert at the *Festspielhaus* on Tuesday. I shall pretend I never opened this door. Kitty, will you join me? Kitty? (KITTY *leaves* GERTRUDE *and goes over to* RAINA *and* HEIDI) Very well. But please, do be careful.

(GERTRUDE *exits and we hear a door close*)

KITTY: Madame Aldric, do not fear, we shall bring you to safe harbor.

(Music comes in, tender and somewhat sad. It slowly builds as we watch the three women in tableau. The lights fade to black.)

ACT I

Scene Four

The schloss. An hour later. KITTY *enters, looks around furtively, and goes to the telephone. She takes a cigarette from a box on the mantle and lights it with a lighter.*

KITTY *(to the operator):* Hallo, Telephonistin, sprechen Sie Englisch? Koennten Sie mich bitte mit jemandem verbinden, der die Sprache spricht? [Hello, operator, do you speak English? Could you connect me with someone who does?] Thank you. . . . Operator, please connect me to Felsenkirk. The number is Bitburg eight, four thousand. Thank you. . . . Hello, is this the Professor? This is the Countess de Borgia.

(From her room at the top of the stairs, LOTTE *comes out and quietly watches)*

KITTY *(continuing, unaware of* LOTTE*):* I'm calling from the schloss of the Baron Von Elsner. I have seen Raina Aldric and Heidi has told me all. I am willing to do anything I can to help. . . . Yes . . . yes . . . But of course . . . Yes, I can do that. Goodbye. *(She hangs up, thinks for a moment, then picks up the phone again)* Operator, the overseas connection . . . Hello, I would like to place a transatlantic trunk call to the United States. Yes, thank you.

(Very softly we start hearing "scary" music. LOTTE, *now starts down the stairs very quietly and slowly to hear better. She gets all the way to the bottom of the stairs before* KITTY *senses her)*

KITTY *(continuing):* Hello, New York, please. The number is Trafalgar six, five–one–hundred . . . Walter Winchell, please. The Countess de Borgia, and make it snappy. . . . Walter, darling, it's Kitty. I'm calling from Germany and, darling, the Deutschland is as dreary as a rotten *bratwurst.* I've got a scoop for you, but you've got to promise to keep it under your hat for a few days. Remember the German actress, Raina Aldric, well, I've just . . . *(For the first time,* KITTY *feels* LOTTE's *presence, still into phone):* I've just . . . I've just remembered that I left the number in my room. I'll . . . I'll call you later. *(Putting out her cigarette,* KITTY *hangs up the phone as* LOTTE *come into the room. Slowly* KITTY *turns and sees* LOTTE. *Both smile at each other)* Hello, Lotte.

LOTTE: I like your scarf. It's so pretty.

(Scary music builds. LOTTE *starts moving toward* KITTY *slowly as the lights fade to black.)*

ACT I

Scene Five

The schloss, an hour later. LOTTE *is onstage holding* KITTY*'s scarf from the last scene. She hears someone knocking and hides it in the cushions of the sofa.* KAREL *enters, looking for someone.*

KAREL: Good afternoon, Fraulein Von Elsner. *(He turns to leave)*

LOTTE: Who were you looking for?

KAREL: The Countess. I am to drive her to the beautician in the village. *(Looks at slip of paper)* Fritzi's Chalet of Beauty.

LOTTE: Well, she changed her mind. She won't be needing the services of a beautician.

KAREL: Thank you, Fraulein, for the information. *(He turns to leave)*

LOTTE *(blocking him):* Don't go, Karel. I want to talk to you.

KAREL: Yes, Fraulein.

LOTTE: Why won't you call me Lotte? I've asked ya a dozen times.

KAREL: It would not be fitting. I am a soldier under your uncle's command.

LOTTE: Screw him. I want you to be my best friend.

KAREL *(nervously)*: I am your friend . . . uh . . . Lotte.

LOTTE *(caressing his chest)*: You know, you're not that much older than me, Karel.

KAREL: You're growing up very fast.

LOTTE *(with dead seriousness)*: Very fast. I'm bleeding regularly.

KAREL *(trying to be encouraging)*: Congratulations.

LOTTE *(perversely flirtatious)*: I have a confession. I've never seen a man's *weiner*. Take it out, I want to see it.

KAREL *(appalled)*: No, Lotte.

LOTTE: Then give me a kiss. *(She kisses him, he wipes it off unconsciously)* Why did you do that for?

KAREL: What?

LOTTE: You wiped off my kiss.

KAREL: I didn't.

LOTTE *(moving into hysteria)*: You did. It's as if I repulsed you. You hate me, don't you?

KAREL: I don't.

LOTTE: You hate and despise me. Well, you'll be very sorry you wiped off my kiss. *(Viciously)* Very sorry indeed!

(The BARON *and the* DOKTOR *enter)*

BARON: Karel, are you waiting for me? What can I do for you?

KAREL *(panicked):* I was to drive the Countess to the village, but I hear she has changed her mind. If there is nothing else, may I go?

BARON: But of course. *Heil Hitler.*

KAREL: *Heil Hitler. (He exits)*

BARON *(furious):* Those blundering idiots! How could a sick, old woman be allowed to escape?

DOKTOR: That sick old woman has strong allies. Do not worry, Raina Aldric's friends shall be rounded up and executed.

LOTTE: Uncle, I have already done . . .

BARON: Death will be too mild. First, in the name of science, they will all be volunteered as subjects for your most extreme medical experiments.

DOKTOR: Science must be served.

LOTTE: Uncle . . .

DOKTOR: Herr Baron, why is this case of such importance to you?

BARON: To the liberals, Raina Aldric is a great symbol of artistic conscience. That symbol must be crushed. Art must serve the nation.

DOKTOR: But Herr Baron, who is to judge what is good or bad art?

BARON *(intrigued):* Such questions, Herr Doktor. You are beginning to sound like a liberal.

DOKTOR *(alarmed):* No, Baron, call me anything but not a liberal.

BARON: Decent people can judge what is obscene. All of the arts are mired in decadence. And the theatre is the worse. I am sick of effeminate neurotics parading their warped fantasies across our stages.

LOTTE: Uncle, listen to me. I have taken care of the little matter you spoke of. One of Raina Aldric's cohorts has indeed been disposed of.

BARON *(pleased):* Lotte, my little bulldog. You have done well. *(He roughhouses with her. She barks like a dog)* Bite the Doktor, Bite the Doktor. Sic him, Lotte, sic him.

(She attacks the DOKTOR like a pit bull)

DOKTOR: Lotte, stop!!! Please stop!!!

(GERTRUDE enters from the front door in riding clothes, brandishing a riding crop)

GERTRUDE *(amused by the spectacle):* Oh dear, I knew I should have packed a muzzle.

BARON: *Liebchen,* have you had a brisk canter?

GERTRUDE *(full of vigor):* Bracing, invigorating. Have you seen Kitty? We're having our hair done together in the village.

BARON: I have not seen her.

LOTTE: I saw her this morning. She did not seem quite herself.

GERTRUDE *(placing her knee on the back of the sofa jauntily)*: Really, in what way?

LOTTE: She mentioned something about an albatross around her neck, choking her. What could she have meant?

DOKTOR: A most stimulating young woman.

BARON: We are going to the beer garden in the village. Care to join us?

GERTRUDE: No, thank you, I think I'll wait for Kitty.

BARON: You should not be alone. But, I imagine loneliness is a cloak worn by all artists.

GERTRUDE: It would take a special man to strip it off me.

BARON *(tantalized)*: Most provocative, Gertrude. Before long I shall find the key to your mysterious nature.

GERTRUDE *(suspicious of his intentions)*: The key?

(They stare at each other for a beat)

BARON: Yes, the key. Till later. *Auf Weidersehen,* my sweet.

(BARON, DOKTOR, *and* LOTTE *exit into library)*

GERTRUDE: *Auf Weidersehen. (She nervously takes the keys from her pocket, checks kitchen door, and tiptoes over to the safe. She swings the portrait open and attempts to open the safe)* Turn three times to zero. Then the opposite way round to twelve and then back to six. *(It doesn't open)* Oh boy. It must have been left round to twelve . . . no . . . it was six . . .

AUGUSTA *(off-stage from kitchen):* No, Elsa, I said *"sauer-braten for six,"* not *at* six.

(GERTRUDE *quickly closes the portrait and puts keys back in her pocket and looks up at portrait as* AUGUSTA *enters, carrying a large book. She is surprised to see* GERTRUDE)

AUGUSTA: Gertrude?

GERTRUDE: I can gaze at this portrait for hours. Those eyes, so sensitive and yet so virile.

AUGUSTA *(in rapture):* What an honor to serve such a man. My only regret is that I am too old to bear him children.

GERTRUDE: There are other forms of volunteer work. Please, don't let me disturb whatever it was you were doing.

AUGUSTA: I was consulting my astrological charts. I find astrology a cruelly neglected science. What is your birthday, Gertrude?

GERTRUDE: August twenty–third. The cusp of Leo and Virgo.

AUGUSTA: A most revealing horoscope *(pronounced* whore–*scope).*

GERTRUDE *(laughing):* That's horoscope, Baroness.

AUGUSTA *(laughing):* My English. Do forgive.

GERTRUDE: Of course.

AUGUSTA: I would imagine you are far closer to the lion than the virgin.

GERTRUDE *(catching her drift):* No, I think I'm right in the middle.

AUGUSTA: A combination is rather interesting. One could be a ferocious prude or a methodical *tramp.*

GERTRUDE *(hardboiled to the core):* Enough with the digs. You don't like me, do you? Why?

(She crosses to AUGUSTA *confrontationally)*

AUGUSTA *(calmly):* Because you are from a hateful enemy nation. You are cheap and common, are using my son and embody everything I loathe in the human race.

GERTRUDE *(beat):* Gimme another reason.

AUGUSTA: Fraulein Garnet, you are a guest of my son. I am doing my best to be gracious to you and your friend. By the way, where is the Countess?

GERTRUDE *(concerned):* I don't know, but I should like to find her.

AUGUSTA *(going upstairs):* Do not worry. I am sure you will find her shortly, my dear. I suppose she could be almost anywhere. Good day.

(AUGUSTA *exits into* LOTTE*'s room. Feeling great anxiety,* GERTRUDE *sits on the sofa. She stretches her arms out and flings them down wide. Accidentally, she touches* KITTY*'s scarf tucked behind a pillow. Tense, suspenseful music underscores the rest of the action. Confused,* GERTRUDE *picks up the scarf. Determined to get to the bottom of* KITTY*'s disappearance, she puts down the scarf and crosses to the stage left arch. She calls out "Kitty!" When there's no response, she crosses center stage and looks up to the landing and calls out "Kitty!" Still no response. Resigned, she slowly crosses to the downstage right door, lost in her thoughts. She opens the door and to her horror,* KITTY *swings out, hanging from a noose, her face hideously contorted.* GERTRUDE *screams, "What have those fiends done to you!" As* KITTY *continues to swing back and forth,* GER-

TRUDE *runs to the mantel to steady herself. In hysteria, she crosses back to* KITTY *and then collapses to the floor in a faint as the music builds to a climax and the lights fade quickly to black.)*

END OF ACT ONE

ACT
TWO

While Raina Aldric (Meghan Robinson, at left) escapes a Nazi prison, Gertrude Garnet (Charles Busch, at right) distracts Baron Von Elsner (Kenneth Elliott) as his niece Lotte (Andy Halliday) looks skeptically on.

Photo by T.L. Boston

ACT II

Scene One

The schloss, several hours later. ERIK *is comforting* GERTRUDE. *She suffers beautifully in a luxurious full length velvet dressing gown.*

GERTRUDE: It was horrible. Her lovely face, so twisted, her eyes bulging.

ERIK: Here, take my handkerchief. Where is she now?

(He gives her his handkerchief, she uses it and returns it to him)

GERTRUDE: I must have fainted. When I came to, her body was gone. Thank you for rushing over so quickly. You must think me totally mad.

ERIK: I believe every word you've said.

GERTRUDE: How could they do this? She who was so kind, so gentle.

ERIK: They'll stop at nothing until the whole world is filled with their evil.

GERTRUDE *(rising from the sofa):* I must see the swami. He'll make sense of this. He says everything happens because we choose it. I must take comfort in that.

ERIK *(challenging her):* Then Kitty somehow wanted to die?

GERTRUDE *(crying out in confusion):* I don't know! She couldn't. No one loved life more than Kitty. Erik, I'm so confused. It's as if the ribbon that's kept my world together has untied. You see, Kitty and I fought. She said I was selfish, that I think only of myself . . . and Erik, she was so right. I've lived a terrible life and now, now I'm so ashamed.

ERIK: I'm sure she would have forgiven you.

GERTRUDE: That I shall never know.

ERIK: I imagine you'll be on the next plane.

GERTRUDE: No, I'm staying on.

ERIK: What do you mean?

GERTRUDE: I must avenge Kitty's death. She was my friend. I must finish the work she died for, saving your mother. The Baron and his henchmen knew of Kitty's pledge to aid your mother. That's why they killed her. Raina Aldric must leave Germany alive.

ERIK: Then you're with us?

GERTRUDE: If you'll have me. I'll cancel my concert at the *Festspielhaus.* I'll whip up some excuse, but first I must see the Baron. I'll have it out with him. Force him to admit they murdered Kitty.

ERIK: No, you must pretend you never found Kitty.

GERTRUDE *(aghast):* But Erik . . .

ERIK *(forcefully):* Listen to what I say. You can do us more good if the Baron continues to trust you.

GERTRUDE: You're asking me to pretend I'm in love with him, aren't you?

ERIK: Yes, I am. It will act as a smokescreen to mask our true plans. Will you do this? Can you do this?

GERTRUDE *(revolted but game):* Yes. You can depend on me. I shall carry out this deception to its very end. Can you ever forgive me for my foolishness?

(Tender, romantic music underscores the scene)

ERIK: Of course. You're so unbelievably beautiful at this moment. The way the sunset catches your face and hair.

GERTRUDE *(composing her face into an unforgettable image):* Oh, you mean like this?

ERIK *(with deadpan thoughtfulness):* No, like this. *(Adjusting the position of her head)* I know it's madness to feel this way after so short a time and with so much at stake, but I love you, Gertie.

GERTRUDE: Please, don't say it.

ERIK: I love you. From the first moment I met you.

GERTRUDE *(tenderly):* I believe you, and the strange thing is, I feel the same. For the first time, something has burst inside me and I feel what the poets call love. But do I trust it?

ERIK: You must and you will.

GERTRUDE *(tremulously):* Erik, hold my hands.

ERIK: Really? I know how you feel about your hands.

GERTRUDE: It doesn't seem to matter anymore. Today, we all need as much tenderness as we can find. *(She takes his hands)* Hold my hands like any American boy would do with his girl. They won't win, will they, darling, the Nazis?

ERIK *(with inspiring fervor):* We won't let 'em. God is on our side. Yeah, he's a regular Joe who won't let the bad guys get away with just a kick in the pants. You'll see, this time the krauts will be smashed to smithereens forever.

GERTRUDE: And will we be fighting alone?

ERIK: No, ma'am. All of Europe will join together. Uncle Sam'll come in swinging, and Russia too. Sure the Nazis fooled 'em for a while, but they've wised up. I met Joe Stalin once, at a seminar in Moscow. He wasn't so bad. Believe me, kiddo, he won't let old Shicklegruber into his backyard.

GERTRUDE: I love hearing you talk this way.

ERIK: I love holding you this way. *(He gently kisses her)*

GERTRUDE: Darling, we have so little time. Do you see that portrait? Behind it lies a safe. This morning, Kit—Kitty and I opened it and found the keys to all the rooms in the house.

ERIK: Good going.

GERTRUDE: Unfortunately, when I tried to return them, I forgot the combination. I'm terrified the Baron will notice the keys are missing.

ERIK: We can only hope he doesn't go near the safe for *(looks at his watch)* for the next six hours. Let's fetch Mother from the catacombs.

GERTRUDE: I've seen to that already. I've hidden your mother and Heidi in the butler's pantry.

ERIK: You're a genius.

GERTRUDE *(radiantly):* Go to her, darling.

ERIK: Mother on the other side of that door. It's been so many years since I've seen her. I've got the willies.

(HEIDI *wheels* RAINA *in from kitchen)*

RAINA: Erik?

ERIK: Mother.

RAINA: My darling. *(They embrace)* I thought I'd never see you again. Look at you, so big, so handsome. You were a little boy when last I saw you.

ERIK: From now on, you'll never be alone.

RAINA: My heart can't take such happiness. My dear, too many years have been wasted. Perhaps it was wrong of me to pursue the career I did, traveling around the world.

ERIK: You're a great artist.

RAINA: Yes, but I had a child. You must believe me, I wanted to take you with me, but your father, the son of a bitch, he thought it best that you grow up in a more normal, stable household. You don't hate me?

ERIK: Hate you? I worship you.

HEIDI: Come, we'd best hurry.

RAINA: Where do we go now?

GERTRUDE: Erik, you and Heidi leave. I'll take care of your mother for the few hours until the car arrives at midnight.

HEIDI: But I couldn't possibly leave her.

RAINA: Heidi, darling, you must do what Madame Garnet says. She knows best.

HEIDI *(near hysterics):* But what if she has another attack or starts to shake or falls into a coma or what if she . . .

RAINA: Heidi—

HEIDI: Yes, ma'am.

GERTRUDE: I'll bring Madame Aldric upstairs to the attic. There is to be a supper party tonight and that should divert attention.

ERIK: It's like you're a different woman.

GERTRUDE: I am a different woman. *(With a swift gesture, she lifts* ERIK's *coat and hat off the back of the sofa)* Come, hurry.

ERIK: Mother, this shall be our last goodbye for a long time.

RAINA: God bless you.

(They kiss)

HEIDI: Goodbye, Madame Aldric.

GERTRUDE: Godspeed.

(She gives coat and hat to ERIK. *He kisses her on the cheek. He and* HEIDI *exit)*

RAINA: He loves you, Madame Garnet.

GERTRUDE *(embarrassed):* Oh.

RAINA: And you love him.

GERTRUDE: Oh.

RAINA: You're blushing. (GERTRUDE, *blushing, makes a raspberry sound and puts her face against the wall)* I'm a worldly woman. I know a great deal about love, particularly how to squander it.

GERTRUDE: We hardly know each other. What we may say now, in a moment of . . .

RAINA: It can happen in an instant. Two people meet and their past and future are one. Don't end up like me, old, sick, alone. Look at this face, look at it. There's a lot of mileage on this puss. Every role I played, every dirty dressing room, every mile I traveled is etched on this map. Look at it, my girl, this could be you.

GERTRUDE *(horrified):* No! No! *(They hear* LOTTE *barking from salon)* Oh my God, someone's coming. Hide behind the sofa.

RAINA: But I can't.

GERTRUDE: Get down.

(She pushes her out of the wheelchair and behind the sofa. The downstage right door to the salon opens, obscuring GERTRUDE as she pushes the wheelchair out the swinging kitchen door)

LOTTE *(as she enters from the salon followed by the* BARON): I hate her. I hate her.

BARON *(following* LOTTE): But, Lotte, you will learn to love Madame—*(Turns as* GERTRUDE *shuts salon door)* Ah, Gertrude! Are you alone in here? I thought I heard voices.

LOTTE: There were two female voices, Uncle.

GERTRUDE: I suppose I'll have to confess. I've been involved in a top secret project.

BARON: Indeed?

GERTRUDE *(madly improvising):* I'm composing an opera. I was acting out all the roles. It's a very contemporary opera.

LOTTE: She's lying. Don't believe her.

BARON: Lotte, that was ill–mannered. Apologize to Madame Garnet.

LOTTE *(crosses to her):* I love stories. Tell us the story of your opera.

GERTRUDE: Never you mind. It's very sophisticated and I wouldn't want your hormones to go haywire. You're liable to wake up in the morning, full–breasted and with a moustache. No, I'm dreadfully tired. I think I'll lie down here for awhile.

BARON: Wouldn't you be more comfortable in your own room?

LOTTE *(very bitchy):* Uncle, I think Madame Garnet would like to be alone in this room. It's so dusty! That new servant girl is so incompetent. Let me do a quick cleanup of the *entire* room.

GERTRUDE *(rushing to LOTTE):* No! It was rude of me not telling you the story of my opera. Let's see. I'll act out the whole thing for you. Lotte, you sit over here. *(She pushes LOTTE down on the sofa with such force that LOTTE's skirt flies up reducing her to a flurry of pink petticoats) (To BARON)* And you, darling, you sit over here. Nice and comfy. *(She gently seats him also on the sofa)* This shall be the stage. *(She indicates the downstage area. She moves down near fireplace*

as RAINA'*s head pops up behind sofa)* It all takes place in
Greenwich Village. That's part of New York. Downtown.
(She sees RAINA) No, what am I saying? I've changed it. It
takes place in Harlem. That's uptown. Up, up, uptown. *(She
points for* RAINA *to go upstairs)* It's the upper corner of
Manhattan Island. The upper right corner. (RAINA *drags
herself up the stairs)* That's right, folks, Harlem. The home of
Jelly–roll Morton, the Cotton Club, Satchmo. *(She sits on
arm of sofa next to the* BARON, *as* RAINA *starts up to the first
landing)* It's about the wild bohemian set. Grasping at everything life has to offer, one step at a time. This woman,
Annabella, is a painter, a painter of large murals and loose
morals. Isn't that funny? Sometimes I just come up with
these little . . . *(No one is laughing)* She falls in love with a
nobleman, kind of like you.

BARON: Like me?

GERTRUDE: Oh yes, handsome, debonair.

BARON: This nobleman, he makes her happy?

GERTRUDE *(near hysteria):* Oh honey, she's downright slap-
   happy!

BARON *(amused):* Then it must be, what you call, escapist entertainment.

GERTRUDE: You might say.

LOTTE *(standing up):* I'm bored.

(RAINA *hides around corner of first landing, as* GERTRUDE
stands up and runs to LOTTE *holding an imaginary knife)*

GERTRUDE *(screams):* A crazy lady runs out of a building holding a knife. She sings "I can't, I can't. I can't go on much
   longer like this." *(During this, she has "stabbed"* LOTTE
   back down on the sofa again. RAINA *falls from her hiding*

place onto the newel post of the second landing) The music gets faster and faster. It speeds up, accelerato! (RAINA *falls onto second landing stairs)* It slows down. (RAINA *drags herself up to second landing)*

BARON *(starting to get up):* It's chilly in here. Let me close the window.

GERTRUDE *(pushing the* BARON *back onto the sofa):* I didn't tell you, Annabella also works as a part–time chiropractor. She met the Baron while cracking his neck.

(She sits between the BARON *and* LOTTE *and with one arm grabs the* BARON *around the neck to keep him from seeing* RAINA)

BARON: Ow!

LOTTE: It *is* cold in here. I'll close the . . .

GERTRUDE *(with her other arm, grabs* LOTTE *around the neck):* She's also a part–time lesbian.

BARON: This sounds like decadent art.

GERTRUDE: Oh, it's madly decadent. Annabella seduces the Baron and his niece. She takes them to her artist's garrett and forces them both to strip naked. *(Behind them on the top landing,* RAINA *realizes she simply can't walk another foot to get to the door. She does a full somersault that gets her to the exit)* Slowly she caresses their nude bodies and . . . (GERTRUDE *looks up and* RAINA *gives her the okay sign, then exits)*

GERTRUDE: And that's all I'm going to tell you. I'm fairly tingling with inspiration. I must go to my room and compose.

(She runs up the stairs at a clip)

BARON: But, Gertrude, what happens next?

GERTRUDE: I'm concentrating, darling.

(She sings strange atonal phrases as she ascends the stairs and exits)

LOTTE: The whole thing was a lie.

BARON: Lotte, you must not be so suspicious. Come, Lotte, let us go to the freezers and choose the best steaks and sausages for tonight's supper.

(They cross to the mantle. The BARON moves Hitler's portrait, revealing the safe)

LOTTE: Oh, Uncle, this is an honor. You've never let me see the freezers before.

BARON: I keep my special keys in the safe behind this portrait. *(Does the combination)* Now that you are a young woman, I shall trust you with these keys. *(Opens the safe, sees keys are missing)* That's strange. The keys are missing.

LOTTE *(gasps):* She took them! She took them! I thought I saw her sneaking around here this morning.

BARON: Who, Lotte?

LOTTE: The piano player, Miss Gertrude Garnet!

BARON: But why should she do this? She is in love with me. True, her friend was a conspirator, but not Gertrude. I don't believe it.

LOTTE: Uncle, only an hour ago I heard her arrange to meet the other American, Erik Maxwell. Are you aware that Erik Maxwell is none other than the son of Raina Aldric?

BARON (*screams and starts to strangle* LOTTE): That is not true!!! (*Controls himself*) Is true. What a great fool I am. What have I done?

(*The* BARONESS AUGUSTA *enters with basket of apples*)

AUGUSTA: Good afternoon, my *liebchen*. Why so glum? It is a gorgeous day.

BARON: *Mutter,* I have done a terrible thing. We must talk.

AUGUSTA (*fearing the worst*): What have you done, Willy?

BARON: It is hard for me to say.

AUGUSTA: First, bring me a cigar. Then you will sit here and tell me what you have done.

(*She sits on sofa, putting basket of apples onto floor*)

BARON: *Mutter,* I have fallen in love. (*Lights cigar*) I have fallen in love with an American agent.

AUGUSTA: Is she with a big agency like William Morris?

BARON: You don't understand. She is a spy. Gertrude Garnet has helped Raina Aldric to escape.

AUGUSTA (*fiercely*): Swine!!! (*Slapping him*) Dumbkopf!! Why do you not listen to me?

BARON: Mother, please.

AUGUSTA: You are weak, Wilhelm, weak. This is the eternal curse of the Von Elsners.

BARON: Please, Mother, not in front of Lotte.

AUGUSTA: No, she must stay. She is more of a man than you. Let her know of her heritage and the cross she must bear. All of the men in your ancient line have been weak, infantile. It is the women who have led the family to greatness.

BARON: That is not true. My father died a hero in battle.

AUGUSTA: Your father died in a madhouse. I should know. I placed him there. They all go the same way. First they display childlike stupidity, then impotence, and then madness.

BARON *(spooked):* I am still not mad. I will show you, Mother. I will show you I am not weak. Fraulein Garnet!!!

AUGUSTA: Don't! I gather she does not know you know that she knows that we know.

BARON: Uh–uh.

AUGUSTA: Then let us wait a bit longer.

LOTTE: And then I will strangle her myself.

AUGUSTA: No, Lotte, that would not look good. Such an important personage must not be found murdered. It must appear far more natural. I shall take care of the lady in question. (BARON *cries, head in hands)* Do not worry, my little Wilhelm, Mother will take care of everything.

(Bright Viennese waltz music comes in as the lights fade to black and continues into the next scene)

ACT II

Scene Two

The schloss, that evening. GERTRUDE, DOKTOR, BARON *and* LOTTE *enter from dinner.* GERTRUDE *carries an evening bag. A small sidetable has been added against the downstage right wall.*

GERTRUDE: Dinner was absolutely superb. The *weinershnitzel* and *sauerbraten* were perfection and the potato dumplings, so delectable. I will not leave without your mother's recipe.

*(*GERTRUDE *sits on the sofa)*

BARON: I am so happy you enjoyed your last supper . . . before you leave us. Is there no way, my darling, I can persuade you to stay?

(He sits next to GERTRUDE *on the sofa)*

GERTRUDE: I'm afraid not. When MGM calls, one lifts one's skirts and runs. Just imagine, me starring as myself in my own musical biography, "I Love a Piano." Of course, I am heartbroken I had to cancel my concert at the *Festspielhaus.* All those poor little burghers who camped out all night to buy their tickets.

LOTTE: But what of your friend, the Countess? What if she returns and you're not here?

GERTRUDE *(holding herself together):* I'm sure wherever she is, she will understand.

BARON: She left without saying goodbye.

DOKTOR *(crossing to fireplace and lights a cigarette):* An enchanting creature.

BARON: But you, Gertrude, when will I see you again?

GERTRUDE: I shall be in Los Angeles through December. I'm sure by then, darling, you and your men will be marching down La Cienega Boulevard.

DOKTOR: I am so disappointed. I did so want to show you my laboratory. I am just beginning with human experiments.

GERTRUDE: I am fascinated by science. Music is, after all, closely allied to the field of physics.

BARON: Perhaps Herr Doktor, Gertrude will stay if we, how do you Americans say, twist her arm.

LOTTE: I'll twist her arm, Uncle.

GERTRUDE: Dear Lotte, I do hope some day you'll realize that you have a special kind of beauty, the kind which comes from within, my precious little monkeyface.

(AUGUSTA *enters with a tray of strudel, through the kitchen's swinging doors. She places it on the small table against the downstage right wall)*

AUGUSTA: I have a surprise for our lovely guest. I have baked my famous Von Elsner *strudel*.

BARON: Oh, Mother, you haven't. Gertrude, we have a great treat in store for us.

GERTRUDE: Oh, dear. Had I but known. The *sauerbraten* did me in.

LOTTE: This *strudel* will really do you in.

GERTRUDE: My girdle is way too tight already.

AUGUSTA: Just a small piece, a sliver.

GERTRUDE: I couldn't.

BARON: Mother shall be quite offended.

AUGUSTA: I shall be furious.

GERTRUDE: I'll take a sliver.

AUGUSTA: The pieces are already cut, so you just eat as much as you can.

(She puts powdered sugar on GERTRUDE's *strudel)*

DOKTOR: Augusta, *I* am furious. Never once have you baked me your famous *strudel*.

AUGUSTA *(serving everyone):* Tut, tut, tut, Herr Doktor. When your first human experiment survives, I shall make you my all–butter pound cake. *(Giving* GERTRUDE *her specially prepared piece of strudel)* Eat up, dear. See if it is to your taste.

GERTRUDE *(innocently perplexed):* Why is mine the only piece with powdered sugar?

AUGUSTA: I . . . I understood all Americans liked things sweet. Should I take it off?

GERTRUDE: No. It looks divine. *(They all stare at her. She takes a bite and grimaces with revulsion then tries to be polite)* Mmmm, light as air.

BARON: Mother, you must have worked hours on that *strudel.*

LOTTE: And I helped.

AUGUSTA: Indeed she did. Lotte was my chancellor of ingredients. And she was most precise, everything according to measure.

(GERTRUDE is gradually growing sicker)

DOKTOR: That powdered sugar looks good.

BARON: Careful, Max. You don't want a pot belly.

DOKTOR: I don't care. Madame Garnet, if you don't mind, I shall be quite boorish and take a little of that powdered sugar.

(GERTRUDE holds out her plate and the DOKTOR's fork is going for the sugar)

BARON *(alarmed):*	AUGUSTA *(fiercely):*
That's for Ger . . .	No, Max . . . sweets are not good for you.

(The DOKTOR pulls back his fork and GERTRUDE realizes there's poison in the sugar. She looks at the DOKTOR)

GERTRUDE *(elegantly):* Excuse me. *(She gives her plate to BARON)* Excuse me. *(She leans over the back of the sofa and violently throws it all up. The others quickly get out of the way)* I guess it didn't agree with me.

AUGUSTA: You have not fooled us, Fraulein Garnet.

(DOKTOR *crosses to a lever against the upstage left wall and pulls it up. A strong "interrogation" light hits* GERTRUDE *on the sofa*)

BARON: Mother, let me handle this. Gertrude, you will tell us everything you know about Raina Aldric.

GERTRUDE: She's a great actress.

BARON: Tell me more.

GERTRUDE: I believe she made a silent film in twenty–six.

BARON *(barking):* Do not be flippant! You have taken me for an idiot, but no more. Your life is in my hands. Raina Aldric has escaped her prison. You have helped her. Who are your confederates?

GERTRUDE *(terrified):* I don't know what you're talking about.

AUGUSTA: Your friend Kitty, she knew, didn't she?

GERTRUDE *(emotionally):* You tell me, since I'm sure you were the last to see her alive.

BARON: Where is Raina Aldric now? Tell me the truth!

GERTRUDE *(fighting for composure):* I don't know where she is. Never met the dame.

DOKTOR: Where is Raina Aldric?

GERTRUDE *(assuming a tough facade):* Don't you guys lissen? I told you I know nothing about that old lady. Got my own troubles, and if Goering, Goebbels and Himmler asked me, I'd tell 'em the same. And get that light out of my eyes. What are you fitting me for, glasses?

AUGUSTA: We will be fitting you for a coffin if you do not comply.

GERTRUDE: Testy.

BARON: Why should you be so loyal to your country? I thought you considered yourself a citizen of the world, Madame Gertrude Gar*net*. [Gar–nay]

GERTRUDE: The name's Gertie Garnet *(in the American pronunciation)* and I'm a citizen of Brooklyn, New York.

DOKTOR: Brooklyn?

GERTRUDE: Yeah, what's it to you?

BARON: This Brooklyn, it will soon be part of the Third Reich.

GERTRUDE *(with defiant pride):* Brother, you may take the Maginot Line, but you'll never take the Canarsie Line.

AUGUSTA: Your bravado is quite pathetic.

GERTRUDE: I give as good as I get.

DOKTOR: You will tell us the truth. I have severe medical methods that can be most excruciating.

GERTRUDE: All right, I'll give you some truth. This whole set–up in Germany stinks. And your Fuhrer, Herr Hitler, has only one nut to his name.

AUGUSTA *(in a rage):* Damn you! Damn you!!!

BARON: Mother, control yourself.

AUGUSTA *(with mad fervor):* That is a filthy lie. The Fuhrer has two enormous testicles!!

BARON: I believe this is time to call in our next subject. Doktor Maximilian, have Karel bring in the young lady.

GERTRUDE: Please don't.

(The DOKTOR *pulls down the lever, killing the light. He calls "*KAREL!*"* KAREL *enters with* HEIDI *and pushes her towards the fireplace.* KAREL *stands behind the sofa)*

BARON: Good evening, Miss Mittelhoffer. So happy you could join us. Please answer a few questions, and then we shall release you. Where is Raina Aldric?

HEIDI *(lying very badly):* I know nothing. Please believe me.

BARON: Come, child, do not fear us. We will not harm you. Where have you taken her?

HEIDI: I know nothing. Please let me go.

BARON: You are guilty of hideous crimes against the Reich. You will tell us everything.

AUGUSTA: Let me. *(She crosses for a cigar)* Miss Mittelhoffer. Do you mind if I call you Heidi? Pardon my indulgence. There's nothing I like better than a good after–dinner cigar. So fragrant. So satisfying. *(Holds the lit cigar close to* HEIDI*'s face)* Tell me, girl, where is Raina Aldric?

HEIDI: Believe me. I don't know where she is.

AUGUSTA: You are very pretty. I can make it so no man will ever love you.

HEIDI *(near hysterics):* Please believe me. I don't know anything.

*(*AUGUSTA, *frustrated, crosses the stage growling like an animal)*

LOTTE: Karel, you're very quiet. Karel and Miss Mittelhoffer are very old friends. Perhaps Karel will have some influence on her.

KAREL: We are mere acquaintances.

LOTTE *(viciously):* That's not true. I believe they were once sweethearts.

BARON: Who is your allegiance to? This tramp or the Fuhrer?

KAREL: The Fuhrer, Herr Baron.

BARON: Then rip off her blouse. Rip it off, I command you.

(KAREL *rips off her blouse, revealing her chemise)*

BARON: Mother, the whip. (AUGUSTA *gets whip from table and gives it to the* BARON) Doktor, please escort Mother to the library. Lotte, go to your room. This is not for your eyes.

LOTTE: Oh drat, just when the fun starts.

(AUGUSTA *and the* DOKTOR *exit upstage left.* LOTTE *runs upstairs and exits)*

BARON *(handing whip to KAREL):* Karel, give her five lashes and perhaps her memory will serve her better.

KAREL *(tortured):*   Yes, Herr Baron.

GERTRUDE *(rushing to the* BARON): Please! The girl is innocent. She has been told nothing.

BARON: Silence!!! Proceed, Karel.

(KAREL *places* HEIDI*'s hands on the mantel of the fireplace to steady her and hesitantly starts to whip her. Each time he hits her, the* BARON *yells, "Harder." Although she screams at each* *strike, she is being* very *brave. On the last one, she falls to the floor sobbing.* KAREL *is in a state of shock)*

BARON: Once more, tell me, girl, where is Raina Aldric?

HEIDI *(with raw, ugly power):* You can all go rot in *hell!!!!*

BARON: How defiant and most entertaining. I am in the mood for more entertainment. Karel, I would like to see you and this young lady have sexual intercourse. Here, before us. Karel, rape her.

KAREL: Please, Baron, do not force me to do this.

BARON: You must do this for the Fuhrer.

KAREL: I can't. I won't! Have you no respect for human life?

BARON: Karel, watch yourself.

KAREL *(taking out a gun and pointing it at the* BARON): No, watch yourself. I thought you were a great man. How wrong I was, you are a monster. Heidi, put on your blouse, we're going.

(LOTTE *enters from upstairs)*

BARON: Where are you going? You fool. Traitor!

LOTTE *(runs down the stairs):* Karel, you're leaving. You're leaving together. You can't do that. You can't do that! I won't let you!

KAREL: Don't come any closer!

LOTTE *(feverishly):* I'm the one you desire.

BARON *(aghast):* Lotte, what are you saying?

LOTTE: Ravage me, impale me!

KAREL: Get out of my way.

LOTTE: Fuck me, Karel, fuck me! *(Insane)* You don't want her. I'll get her out of the way. I'll kill her for you. This will be the test of my love.

(She pulls out a knife and is about to stab HEIDI *when* KAREL *shoots her and she falls dead)*

KAREL *(dropping the gun on the sofa in disgust):* Come, Heidi.

(They run out the front door)

BARON *(with mad vengeance):* The traitors, they will not go far. I shall phone the Gestapo and put an end to this ridiculous love story.

*(*GERTRUDE *picks up the gun from the sofa and points it at him)*

GERTRUDE: Put down that phone.

BARON: I certainly will not.

GERTRUDE: Put it down, I say.

BARON: Give me the gun. You do not have the courage to fire it.

GERTRUDE: Oh, don't I? *(Defiant music comes in)* What a joy it will be to kill you. Yes, joy. But first, I shall torture you as you have tortured thousands. You thought I loved you. I never loved you. I pitied you because you were a pathetic, mother–fixated fool. Imagine my happiness when I execute you and escape with my lover. Yes, my handsome, young lover. You, who hounded an innocent actress nearly to her death. You, who cruelly humiliated a pair of young lovers. You, who murdered my friend. The Lord God in heaven may forgive you, but I never shall. Now die, your excellency, die.

BARON: Gertie, perhaps I was a trifle brusque. *(She pushes him up the stairs. The* BARON *continues, pathetically yellow):* You are a great artist, artists should be above such nonsense as politics. Gertie, don't shoot. I beg of you. I don't wanna die. I'll do anything. I'll make any phone call. I have money. You want cash? How much, take it, a hundred marks? Don't, Gertie, don't. Mother! Mother! Don't shoot.

(She impassively shoots him twice, then once more as an afterthought. The music fades out)

GERTRUDE *(with bitter irony):* And to think, before you once trembled all of Schauffehausen.

ERIK *(running in from the library):* Gertie, are you all right? What happened?

GERTRUDE *(terribly shaken):* I killed him. I killed him.

ERIK: We must get Mother out. The car will be here any minute.

GERTRUDE: What about the Baroness and the Doktor? Shan't they hear us?

ERIK: Dr. Maximilian saw me climbing in through the window. We thrashed it out and I've got him tied up in the basement.

GERTRUDE: And the Baroness . . . ?

ERIK *(lights a cigarette at the mantel):* She heard us fighting and came after me with a shovel. I belted her in the stomach, got her in a half–Nelson and wrestled her to the ground. Then I grabbed her by the hair and dragged her across the room and slammed her against an old chifferobe. When she was knocked out cold, I tied her to the Doktor. They'll keep for a while. Professor Mittelhoffer!

(The PROFESSOR comes in through the front door. ERIK puts out the cigarette)

PROFESSOR: I heard shooting. Was Heidi here? *(Sees the bodies) Ach du leiber.*

GERTRUDE: They brought her in and tortured her. You'd have been proud. They couldn't break her spirit. Karel saved her and got her out of the house. He's on our side now.

PROFESSOR: She is a smart girl, she knows to meet us outside the servants' entrance at midnight. It's almost time.

ERIK: Let's go get Mother. (RAINA *enters from the upstairs right room, walking slowly. She is wearing a fur coat and looks radiant)* Mother, you're walking. *(He starts for her)*

RAINA *(with great courage):* Don't help me. I must walk to freedom on my own two legs!

(They embrace on the stairs)

PROFESSOR: Oh dear, with Karel along, we don't have enough letters of transit. What should we do?

GERTRUDE: Then you must take mine. *(She gets her purse from sofa)*

ERIK: We couldn't. You'd never get out.

GERTRUDE: I'd find a way. I always do.

ERIK *(crossing to the mantel):* We're close to the Swiss border. We could possibly make it by foot.

GERTRUDE: But you, you have a letter of transit.

ERIK: It means nothing without you. I'll take my chance with you in the mountains.

PROFESSOR: It's midnight. I think I hear the car.

RAINA: Bless you, Gertrude. You have given me back my life, my son and my art. "Gallop apace, you fiery–footed steeds . . ."

PROFESSOR: Come, Raina, the plane leaves promptly in ten minutes.

GERTRUDE: Here is your letter of transit, Madame Aldric, and you can't greet your public without this. *(She gives her a lipstick)*

RAINA: A lipstick, and such a lovely color. *(She puts it on, kisses* GERTRUDE's *hands)* Thank you, thank you, thank you.

(GERTRUDE *gives her the handbag)*

ERIK: Mother, I'll meet you across the border. *(They kiss)* Professor, good luck.

(RAINA *and the* PROFESSOR *exit)*

GERTRUDE: Darling, there's still time. You should have gone with them. I'll never forgive myself if you . . .

ERIK: Shhhh. *(They listen to the outside. We hear the car drive off)* They're on their way.

GERTRUDE: What do we do now? How do we find Switzerland?

ERIK: We have very simple directions. I'll show you. *(He takes her hands and leads her to the open door. They look out)* We just follow that brightest star. Are you game?

GERTRUDE: I love an adventure.

ERIK: Let's go.

(Fade to black. Lush, romantic music redolent of courageous adventure comes in and eventually underscores the following voice-over)

ACT II

Scene Three

VOICE–OVER *(in the blackout):* Flash. Flash. Dateline Bavaria. Famed U.S. piano virtuoso, Gertrude Garnet, is missing and feared dead after aiding the escape of German stage actress, Raina Aldric, from a Nazi prison. Miss Aldric and companions have landed safely in Zurich, but fear Nazi retaliation against Miss Garnet and against Miss Aldric's son, Erik Maxwell. Stay tuned for further reports.

(The large screen from Scene One is across the stage. Lights come up on the right side of the screen detailing a mountain landscape. On grooves carved into the screen, two small figurines representing GERTRUDE *and* ERIK *are seen skiing down the mountain. The effect should be that of a movie "long shot." This is accompanied by thrilling adventure music. The lights fade down and rise on the left side of the stage where* GER-TRUDE *and* ERIK *are seen in person skiing on a small slope. Snow is falling on them and loud gunshots are heard in rapid succession)*

GERTRUDE *(skiing):* Faster, darling, faster!

ERIK: Where'd you learn to ski?

GERTRUDE: San Moritz, Vale and Aspen. They're shooting at us!

ERIK: Don't look back! When we get back to the States, will you marry me?

GERTRUDE: Of course, darling. I think I'd make a divine professor's wife. And when I go on tour during summer vacation, will you join me?

ERIK: I'll carry all the luggage.

GERTRUDE: Then you've got yourself a deal. Are we almost there?

ERIK: I can't tell in this darkness.

(A shot rings out and hits ERIK *in the back. He falls to the ground.* GERTRUDE *stops skiing and joins him on the ground. The music and snow fade out)*

GERTRUDE: Erik! Erik!

ERIK: Keep going!

GERTRUDE: I will not. You're hurt. Hold on to me!

ERIK *(through his pain):* No, go ahead. I'll catch up with you.

GERTRUDE *(with great emotion):* Darling, if this is the way it ends, so be it. During these past few days, you've taught me more than most people learn in a lifetime.

ERIK *(fading away):* I can hardly see your face.

GERTRUDE *(desperately):* Hold on to me, darling. *(With great determination)* No one's going to harm you. *(The end seems to be near. Wistful, quietly sad music is heard)* Erik, what a fool I've been. All these years I've been obsessed with myself and called it a philosophy. *(Very simply and with great restraint)* This is what matters. This is real. Fighting for something I believe in. Loving someone. Why must we always come to our senses when it's too late? *(She pauses and realizes there is silence)* Listen, the shooting has stopped. Do you hear?

(ERIK *lifts himself up to a somewhat seated position. He's going to live. The music becomes more hopeful)*

ERIK: Yes, the night is suddenly peaceful.

GERTRUDE *(pointing to the sky):* Look, darling, the brightest star. It's directly over our heads. We must have crossed the border! *(Elated)* We're free, darling, we're free! *(Eyes full of tears, she's the embodiment of bravery as she cradles ERIK in her arms. Her voice rises in emotional rhythm and cadence)* And soon that bright star will shine above all of Europe and the whole world will glow in its radiance, brighter and stronger than we've ever, ever known!

(The music builds triumphantly as the lights fade out on GER-TRUDE and ERIK's upturned, enraptured faces. Above them, we see the snow capped mountains and the title "The End" appears as if through the clouds. Fade to black.)

THE END

PSYCHO BEACH PARTY opened at the Players Theatre in New York City on July 20, 1987. It was directed by Kenneth Elliott. Scenic Design was by B.T. Whitehill, costume design by John Glaser, lighting design by Vivien Leone and wig design by Elizabeth Katherine Carr, who also acted as Production Stage Manager. Original music was composed by Tom Kochan and the choreography was by Jeff Veazey. T.L. Boston was Production Advisor and Julie Halston and Mario Andriolo were Associate Producers.

The cast was as follows:

Yo Yo	Robert Carey
Dee Dee	Judith Hansen
Nicky	Mike Leitheed
Provoloney	Andy Halliday
Star Cat	Arnie Kolodner
Chicklet	Charles Busch
Kanaka	Ralph Buckley
Berdine	Becky London
Marvel Ann	Michael Belanger
Mrs. Forrest	Meghan Robinson
Bettina Barnes	Theresa Marlowe
Swing/Understudy	Laurence Overmire

Time: 1962
Place: On and around a beach in Malibu.

The "Chicklet" love theme was sung by Michael Maguire; lyrics by Ken Elliott.

AUTHOR'S NOTE

Why would anyone want to write a spoof of beach party movies? Well, for one thing, the original "Gidget" movie is not bad. It's not "Le Grand Illusion," but it is fun and insightful, and the movie's star, Sandra Dee, I believe, is a much-maligned talent. Still, a parody of 1960s teen exploitation flicks would seem to be rather thin stuff. I confess, I began writing this play with a fairly crass motive. I needed a vehicle for my theatrical troupe, Theatre-in-Limbo, to perform as a midnight show. One night over pepperoni pizza, off the top of my head, I came out with the title "Gidget Goes Psychotic." I knew right away that that title would pull in our cult audience in droves. You see what I mean, pretty crass thinking.

However, I found while I was writing that by placing Gidget into the genre of psychological melodrama such as "The Three Faces of Eve," "Suddenly Last Summer" and "Spellbound," I was developing something far more interesting. The movie parody was merely a starting point for me to write something rather personal and reflective. I'm hardly attributing Beckettian resonances to "Psycho Beach Party," but I like to think there is more to it than meets the eye. Eventually, I changed the title because I felt "Gidget Goes Psychotic" too specific and limiting.

We found it best to act the play very "straight" and uncampy, but in a heightened emotional style. Some of the biggest laughs came about by an actor reacting in a harrowingly intense manner which was unfortunately inappropriate to the situation. In the original production, I played Chicklet in drag and another fella, Michael Belanger, played Marvel Ann. We tried to play these female roles with total conviction, finding humor in the reality of the character. I don't think it's necessary for men to play these female roles. In fact, my understudy was a girl and played the role very successfully. It was a cruel awakening because I was so sure that I was irreplaceable. I guess you can't be sure of anything in this world. Nothing is what it seems. Like, hey, maybe that's what this play's all about.

PRODUCTION NOTES

Pace is very important to the success of PSYCHO BEACH PARTY. Movement from scene to scene should be fast, in the manner of cinematic quick cuts. Long scene changes will destroy the fluidity of the show.

Although the show is set in a number of locations in and around Malibu, the setting for the New York production was extremely simple. It consisted of a series of decorative portals and a backdrop framing a bare stage. Changes in time and locale were indicated mostly through lighting. There were additional set pieces for some of the scenes which were easily and quickly swung into place. For the last scene, a romantic roll drop depicting a sunset over the Pacific was brought in.

Music is an important element of the show for bridges, underscoring, and musical numbers. The "Luau" scene should open with a wild limbo number. Obviously, the music should be of the early sixties period. Some of the show music from the New York production is available for rental from Samuel French, Inc. But regardless of whether you use the original music or choose your own, it should be remembered that music will help give the show a period flavor and an energetic feeling.

In the original production I played Chicklet in drag. As I've said, this is not necessary. With a girl in the role, one cut in the script is advised.

Scene One

BERDINE: You will, you will.

MARVEL ANN: We're in luck. Look at those four gorgeous hunks of male, over there, almost enough for second helpings. Now, a maneuver like this takes technique. Talk to me. Don't let them think we're looking at them.

Would-be surfer girls Berdine (Becky London), Chicklet (Charles Busch) and Marvel Ann (Michael Belanger) wave to the wave-masters.

Photo by Adam Newman

Scene One

Malibu Beach, 1962. Two handsome, young beach bums named YO YO *and* NICKY, *and a sexy chick in a bikini named* DEE DEE, *are madly cavorting with a beach ball.*

YO YO *(to* DEE DEE): Baby, shake those maracas.

DEE DEE *(squeals):* Stop teasing me, Yo Yo.

NICKY: Look at that butt.

DEE DEE: You guys have a one track mind.

(PROVOLONEY, *a scrappy little surfer, the joker of the group, runs on)*

PROVOLONEY: Girls! Girls! Girls!

YO YO: Hey there, Provoloney!

NICKY and DEE DEE: Hi, Provoloney.

PROVOLONEY: What a fantabulous day.

DEE DEE: Gosh, I love the sun.

NICKY: Aw shoot, we've got to get back to the malt shop. Our lunch break is almost over.

YO YO: Call in sick.

PROVOLONEY: Say you were run over by a hit-and-run surfer.

NICKY: Nah, old Augie's a great guy. I couldn't let him down.

DEE DEE: Gosh, I really love him.

(STAR CAT, *the most handsome of the group, enters with a surfboard*)

YO YO: Hey, Star Cat, how's my man?

STAR CAT: What are you clowns doing? Those waves are as high as Mount Everest.

PROVOLONEY *(looks out):* Oh wow, look at them, man.

STAR CAT: It's time to hit the water.

NICKY: It's more BLTs for us. Let's hit the road, Dee Dee.

DEE DEE: Sure thing. Gosh, I'm so happy. *(They exit)*

BOYS: Bye!

STAR CAT: Come on guys, grab your boards, it's time to shoot the curl.

PROVOLONEY: Hot diggity! *(They all run offstage)*

(CHICKLET, *a perky, fifteen-year-old girl skips on*)

CHICKLET *(to the audience):* Hi folks, welcome to Malibu Beach. I hope you brought your suntan lotion cause here it's what you call endless summer. My name's Chicklet. Sort of a kooky name and, believe me, it has nothing to do with chewing gum. You see, I've always been so darn skinny, a stick, a shrimp, so when other girls turned into gorgeous chicks, I became a chicklet. Can't say I've always been thrilled with that particular nomenclature, but it sure beats the heck out of my real name, Florence. I'm supposed to meet my girlfriends, Marvel Ann and Berdine, here at the beach. Marvel Ann calls it a "man hunt." I don't know what's wrong with me. I like boys, but not when they get all icky and unglued over you. All that kissy kissy stuff just sticks in my craw. I don't know, maybe I need some hormone shots. I do have a deep, all-consuming passion. The mere thought fills me with tingles and ecstasy. It's for surfing. I'm absolutely flaked out about riding the waves. Of course, I don't know how to do it, not yet, but I'm scouting around for a teacher and when I do, look out world. You'll be seeing old Chicklet flying over those waves like a comet.

(KANAKA, *the macho king of the surfers, enters, drinking from a coffee mug)*

CHICKLET: I can't believe it. You're the great Kanaka, aren't you?

KANAKA: Yes, I am the party to whom you are genuflecting.

CHICKLET: Oh gosh, I'm just like your biggest fan. I was standing down front during the surfing competition—

KANAKA: Hey, cool down. Pour some water on that carburetor.

CHICKLET: I haven't even introduced myself, I'm Chicklet Forrest. You're like a living legend. Did you really ride the killer wave off the coast of Bali?

KANAKA: In handcuffs. So how come you know so much about surfing?

CHICKLET: I don't, but I'm dying to learn.

KANAKA: A girl surfer? That's like a bad joke.

CHICKLET: Why? Couldn't you teach me? I'm a great swimmer.

KANAKA: You're a tadpole. You're not meant to hit the high waves. It's like a mystical calling. Sorry, babe, sign up with the YMCA.

CHICKLET: But Kanaka . . .

KANAKA: Hey, little girl. I'm drinking my morning java, my gray cells are still dozing, in other words, angel, buzz off.

BERDINE *(offstage):* Chicklet! Come on!

CHICKLET: Well, you haven't heard the last of me. You'll see, I'm going to be your greatest student if it kills you. Tootles. *(She exits)*

(STAR CAT, YO YO *and* PROVOLONEY *run on, excited)*

STAR CAT: Hey Kanaka! You won't believe what's going on.

PROVOLONEY: I swear Malibu Mac is going to kill the joker.

KANAKA: I'm trying to drink my mother–lovin' java . . .

YO YO: Didn't you see the cop cars down the beach?

KANAKA *(sees them):* Oh yeah, what's happening?

STAR CAT: It's like a bad dream. Malibu Mac has been dating that high school chick, Beverly Jo.

KANAKA: The homecoming queen, right?

PROVOLONEY: They spent the night on the beach.

YO YO: They were knocked out cold.

STAR CAT: This morning they woke up, naked as they were born and some weirdo had shaved their bodies head to toe.

YO YO: Not a whisker on 'em. Twin bowling balls.

KANAKA: And Malibu Mac had a thing about his pompadour.

PROVOLONEY: He looks like a six-foot wiener.

YO YO: Talking about wieners, my stomach's saying "Feed me."

STAR CAT: You're always stuffing your face.

YO YO: Food is my hobby.

PROVOLONEY: Yo Yo's a great chef. We've set up like a whole kitchen in our beach shack.

KANAKA: Our beach shack? I never heard of two surf bums shacking up together.

PROVOLONEY: You should see how Yo Yo has fixed up the place with fishnet curtains, rattan furniture, hanging plants.

KANAKA: Hanging plants?

YO YO (innocently): I do wonderful things with Hibithcuth. (They all do a take)

PROVOLONEY: My innards are screaming, "Chow."

YO YO: Mine are screaming, "Give me chili dogs!"

STAR CAT: See you clowns later.

PROVOLONEY *(exiting with* YO YO): Food! Food! Food! *(They exit)*

STAR CAT: Kanaka, I talked to my dad yesterday.

KANAKA: Yeah?

STAR CAT: I told him I wasn't going back to college. This pre-med stuff is for squares.

KANAKA: But I thought you wanted to be a psychiatrist.

STAR CAT: I was a kid. Now I know I want to be a surf bum. My dad hit the roof, but he doesn't understand. He grew up dirt poor and made his money tooth and nail. I can't compete with that. More than anything I want his respect and I'll get that by bumming around with you.

KANAKA: But you know, being a surf bum is a tall order. Only a few make the grade. It's like being a high priest, kinda. No involvements, no commitments, just following the sun. You gotta be a man.

STAR CAT: I swear I won't let you down.

KANAKA: You're a good guy, Star Cat. I think this is the time I show you some of my treasures. I got in my shack a necklace composed of genuine human eyeballs presented to the great Kanaka by a witch doctor in Peru.

STAR CAT: Oh wow!

KANAKA: Let's go.

(They exit. MARVEL ANN *and* BERDINE *enter carrying beach bags.* MARVEL ANN *is a gorgeous blond high school vamp and* BERDINE *is a hopeless nerd, but a nerd with spunk)*

MARVEL ANN: Honestly, Berdine, did you have to put that disgusting white gook all over your nose?

BERDINE: Sorry, Marvel Ann, but I got this allergy that flares up whenever I go to the beach.

MARVEL ANN: What are you allergic to?

BERDINE: The sun. It's ghastly. My face turns beet red, my eyes close up, and I get this terrible chafing between my legs.

MARVEL ANN: Charming. Help me spread out the blanket. *(They do)*

BERDINE: Marvel Ann, this blanket is really divoon.

MARVEL ANN: It's coordinated with my skin tone. Chicklet, help us.

(CHICKLET *enters*)

CHICKLET: I found something in the sand.

BERDINE: What is it, a shell?

CHICKLET: No, look. *(She dangles a spider in front of* MARVEL ANN*)*

MARVEL ANN *(screaming in terror):* A black widow! *(She pushes it out of* CHICKLET*'s hand)*

CHICKLET: You scared it.

MARVEL ANN: Listen you two weirdos, my nerves are a frazzle. I can't believe what happened to Beverly Jo. I'm going to have nightmares all night from seeing her like that.

BERDINE: I wonder what the penalty is for shaving someone's head.

CHICKLET: It wasn't just her head. Couldn't you see, they also shaved her . . . *(She whispers "pussy" in* BERDINE's *ear and they are dissolved in giggles)*

MARVEL ANN: Cut that out. I think you two have forgotten the reason we're here. This is a man hunt, *capiche?*

CHICKLET: Why do we have to bother with them? Can't we just have a good time by ourselves?

MARVEL ANN: You have a severe problem, Chicklet. You've got the sex drive of a marshmallow, you're pushing sixteen. So what if you're an A student, that's parent's stuff. Get with it.

CHICKLET: Maybe I'm just some kind of a freak. Maybe I'll never fall in love.

BERDINE: Oh you will, you will.

CHICKLET: But how will I know when it hits me?

BERDINE: You will, you will.

MARVEL ANN: Chicklet, what are you trying to do, spoil the picture? Take off your top. You've got your swim suit on, don't you? Peel, girl, peel.

CHICKLET: Darn it, it's in my bag and there's no ladies room to change in.

MARVEL ANN: There's no one around. You better hurry.

BERDINE: You can't take your top off here.

CHICKLET: Hold the blanket up and no one will see me. *(They hold up the blanket,* CHICKLET *takes off her smock, re-*

vealing her nude, flat chest) I'm hopeless. I'm built just like a boy. I wonder if I'll ever fill out.

BERDINE: Hurry up, Chicklet. Marvel Ann, hold the blanket up so I can help Chicklet with her top. (CHICKLET *pulls on her bathing suit top)*

MARVEL ANN: We're in luck. Look at those four gorgeous hunks of male, over there, almost enough for second helpings. Now a maneuver like this takes technique. Talk to me. Don't let them think we're looking at them.

CHICKLET: What should we talk about?

MARVEL ANN: Anything.

BERDINE: I'm reading the most exciting book. It's by Jean Paul Sartre. It's called "Nausea."

MARVEL ANN *(posing and not paying attention):* Oh, really.

BERDINE: It's the most clear-headed explanation of existentialism. The whole concept of free will being conscious choice against the determining . . .

MARVEL ANN *(with extreme bitchiness):* I'll see the movie.

CHICKLET: Gosh, Berdine, I'm impressed. You're a real egghead.

MARVEL ANN: They're looking this way. Now very slowly, let's turn our heads in their direction. *(They simultaneously turn their heads)* Slowly. Cock your head to the side and give a little smile. *(They cock their heads and smile in unison)* Not like that, Berdine, you look like you've got whiplash. (BERDINE *straightens up)* The blond one is giggling. *(She giggles)*

CHICKLET: What's so funny?

MARVEL ANN: Shut up. Now we go in for the kill. *(She makes a sexy growl)*

CHICKLET: What's she doing now?

BERDINE: I believe she's displaying animal magnetism. (BERDINE *and* CHICKLET *start growling and barking like wild dogs and apes)*

MARVEL ANN: What the hell are you two doing? Oh, now you've done it. They're laughing at us. How dare you? I hate you both.

CHICKLET: Marvel Ann, don't lose your sense of humor.

MARVEL ANN *(stands up):* Oh, I'm laughing all right and so is everyone else at school, laughing at how backward you are. I ought to get the purple heart just for being seen with you. *(Turns to leave)*

BERDINE: Where are you going?

MARVEL ANN: I didn't come to the beach to play. I came here to catch a man. So if you'll excuse me, I think I'll set my traps elsewhere.

CHICKLET: Can we come too?

MARVEL ANN: What's the point in meeting boys? You two queerbaits should get a license and marry each other. *(She exits, laughing)*

CHICKLET: What sort of nasty crack is that?

BERDINE: I don't see anything wrong with having a best friend.

CHICKLET: I suppose some friends get so close that they lose their individual identities.

BERDINE: We're two very independent personalities.

CHICKLET: She's just jealous cause . . .

BERDINE *(finishing her sentence):* we've never really accepted her. How could we, she's . . .

CHICKLET: dumb as a stick. I don't think she's ever read a book . . .

BERDINE: all the way to the end. Someday she'll be sorry . . .

CHICKLET: that she rushed into adulthood. We're much wiser to

BERDINE AND CHICKLET *(simultaneously):* take our time.

CHICKLET: I don't think virginity is such a horrible . . .

BERDINE: degrading . . .

CHICKLET: awful thing. You know of course what she did with you know who in the . . .

BERDINE *(understands perfectly):* Uh huh. Uh huh. And did you know she . . .

CHICKLET *(understands perfectly):* Uh huh. But I think there's more to it. I think, well . . . you know . . .

BERDINE: Really? *(Giggles)*

CHICKLET: It reminds me of that book we read, what was it?

BERDINE *(knows the book):* Yes, yes, yes. That's exactly the same kinda . . .

CHICKLET: And look what . . . well . . .

BERDINE: So true, so true. I couldn't have said it better myself.

(MARVEL ANN *enters with* KANAKA *and* STAR CAT)

MARVEL ANN: Look what I found in the sand. Two hunks of California he-man.

KANAKA: I dig a mermaid whose lips are as flip as her fins.

MARVEL ANN *(coyly):* Don't swim too fast upstream, you can still lose the race.

KANAKA: I know how to glide on wave power when I have to.

STAR CAT *(to* MARVEL ANN): Hey, the waves are flipping out. Come and watch me surf standing on my head.

CHICKLET *(wildly impressed):* Can you really do that?

STAR CAT: Sure. *(To* MARVEL ANN) I can do lots of special tricks.

CHICKLET *(innocently):* Really? Like what?

STAR CAT *(to* MARVEL ANN): You interested?

MARVEL ANN *(provocatively):* Very interested.

CHICKLET *(thinks they're talking about surfing):* So am I. Let's go right now.

MARVEL ANN: I'd rather see you try those stunts on land.

CHICKLET: That's not the same thing at all.

MARVEL ANN: I missed your name, tall, dark and brooding.

STAR CAT: They call me Star Cat.

MARVEL ANN: I call you cute.

STAR CAT: I'd like to call you sometime.

MARVEL ANN: I'm in the phone book under my father's name, Franklin McCallister, I'm Marvel Ann.

CHICKLET: You can call me too. I'm Chicklet. Here. I'll write down my number cause, golly, I'd do anything to see you surf standing on your . . .

MARVEL ANN: Oh pooh, the sun's playing hookey. No use sitting around here.

KANAKA: Star Cat, let's help the lady.

STAR CAT: You bet!

MARVEL ANN *(she holds up the blanket, the boys help her)*: Why thank you, gentlemen. Come, girls.

CHICKLET: That's okay, Marvel Ann. I think I'll stay out a little longer. I'll call you when I get home, Berdine. Okle dokle?

BERDINE *(wary)*: Okle dokle.

MARVEL ANN *(suspiciously)*: Okle dokle. *(They exit.)*

KANAKA *(to STAR CAT)*: Good going, pal. I bet she's hot and spicy between the enchilada.

CHICKLET: If Kanaka won't teach me to surf, will you? I'm a quick study. Straight As in all my classes.

STAR CAT: You think I'm impressed? Listen little girl, surfing is a man's work. Be a girl. You're more fish than dish. Me teach you how to surf? Don't make me laugh. I'd rather teach a chicken to lay an elephant's turd. Go home to mama and run, don't walk. *(He exits)*

CHICKLET: Boy, he's a grump.

KANAKA: Aw, Star Cat's a raw pearl. He's just a sensitive kind of fella. Hey, look at that kite.

CHICKLET: Which one?

KANAKA: The red one with the flying fish.

(CHICKLET*'s face becomes distorted and she becomes her alter ego,* ANN BOWMAN, *a glamourous femme fatale)*

KANAKA *(oblivious):* When I was a kid, I was bananas over flying kites. More than anything, I'd like to be running with a kite against the wind.

CHICKLET *(laughs):* Darling, more than anything, I'd like a cool martini, dry with a twist.

KANAKA: Say what?

CHICKLET: You do know what a martini is, my delicious Neanderthal.

KANAKA: Chicklet?

CHICKLET *(laughs):* I'm afraid you've got the wrong girl. Chicklet is not my name.

KANAKA: Who are you?

CHICKLET: My name is Ann Bowman.

KANAKA *(laughs):* That's pretty good. You wanna be an actress?

CHICKLET: I'm revealing my true nature. *(Fingers his fly)* I'd like to see you strip down to your truest self.

KANAKA *(pushes her hand away):* Hey, you shouldn't do that.

CHICKLET: Give me one good reason.

KANAKA: You're underage.

CHICKLET: My energy is as old as the Incan temples. You ever been to Peru, baby?

KANAKA: Can't say I have.

CHICKLET: Someday, you and I must explore the ancient temple of Aca Jo Tep. But enough about that for now, what about us?

KANAKA: Hey, cool your jets, babe. If I didn't live by my personal code of honor, I might take advantage of this situation erotically, as it were.

CHICKLET: Give into the feeling, Daddy-O.

KANAKA: Cut the soundtrack for a minute and listen up. Let me give you the number one rule of sexual relations. No stud digs a heavy come-on from a babe. A chick can play it tough, but underneath the makeup, a dude's gotta know the chick's a lady. In straight lingo, no pigs need apply.

CHICKLET *(lies on the ground):* Forget the rules, lie here on the sand with me. Doncha love the feel of hot sand against your nude flesh?

KANAKA: I don't know what you're up to, but you've got the wrong hep cat.

CHICKLET: Perhaps I do. I thought you were the man with the big cigar. What are you packing, a tiparillo?

KANAKA: More than you can handle, kid. They ought to send you to the juvenile detention hall.

CHICKLET: Aw, I'm scaring the "wittle" boy.

KANAKA: Doll, when I dance, I make the moves, the chick always follows. *(He turns to leave)*

CHICKLET *(with mad ferocity):* Don't you turn your butt to me!

KANAKA *(turns around shocked):* Chicklet?

CHICKLET: I am not Chicklet, you lobotomized numbskull!!!

KANAKA: C'mon, stop fooling.

CHICKLET: Do not test me. I will have my way. *(Laughs)* I frighten you, don't I?

KANAKA: No, I ain't scared.

CHICKLET: You're lying. You're yellow as a traffic light, you sniveling little prick. You're scared.

KANAKA: No.

CHICKLET: Look at your hands, they're shaking like jello.

KANAKA *(hides his hands):* No, they ain't.

CHICKLET: You're scared. Say it, you're scared.

KANAKA: Yes!

CHICKLET: Yes what?

KANAKA: Yes, ma'am.

CHICKLET: Ah, that's better. You're just a little slave boy, aren't you, sonny?

KANAKA: I gotta get outta here.

CHICKLET: You ain't going anywhere, punk. You know, I'm going to give you what you always wanted.

KANAKA: You are?

CHICKLET: I think we understand each other very well. I know what you fantasize about, I know what you dream about and I'm going to give it to you in spades. Now I want you to go into town and buy yourself a slave collar and a garter belt and a pair of black silk stockings. Spike heels will complete the ensemble and then my dear darling Kanaka, I'm gonna shave all that man fur off you and you'll look just like the little boy that you are.

KANAKA: But what will the rest of the fellas think?

CHICKLET (in a rage): To hell with the rest of the fellas! I am the most important! Me! Ann Bowman! I will not be cast aside, I will not be . . . (Becomes CHICKLET again) Of course, my Mom's an old prude, she won't think surfing is ladylike, but I know I can win her over.

KANAKA (in shock): What?

CHICKLET: My Mom. I'm gonna have to ask her permission.

KANAKA: Ann?

CHICKLET: My name's Chicklet, silly. So are you gonna teach me, please, please, pretty please?

KANAKA: Do you remember what we were just talking about?

CHICKLET: Surfing lessons.

KANAKA: No, after that. I mean, before that.

CHICKLET: Your friend Star Cat? I'm wearing down your resistance, aren't I?

KANAKA *(very confused)*: Yeah, I'll say.

CHICKLET: Can we start tomorrow?

KANAKA: Yeah, sure.

CHICKLET: Yippee! I gotta get moving, gotta round up a board, get my Mom's okay and then tomorrow, we hit the old H20. Tootles. *(She exits)*

KANAKA *(scratching his head in disbelief)*: A red kite with a flying fish.

(Blackout.)

Scene Two

CHICKLET's *house. She enters.*

CHICKLET: Mom, I'm home. Gosh, the place looks spotless. Was Sadie here today?

(MRS. FORREST *enters, the spitting image of Joan Crawford)*

MRS. FORREST: Unfortunately no. Poor Sadie's brother Bubba was run over by a hit-and-run driver. You know our Sadie, always an excuse not to work. I've been on my hands and knees scrubbing all morning. And to top it off, I was experimenting, cooking a veal scallopini in the pressure cooker. The darn thing exploded and I'm still finding bits of scallopini in my wiglet.

CHICKLET: Well, the house looks swell.

MRS. FORREST: Thank you, dear. Did you enjoy yourself at the beach? *(Puts arm around her)*

CHICKLET: I guess so.

MRS. FORREST: I detect a sphinx-like expression. Penny for your thoughts.

CHICKLET *(looking for a way to tell her about surfing):* I just hate thinking of you doing all that nasty housework. You're so beautiful.

MRS. FORREST *(laughs):* My darling daughter, I am just an old widow and a little hard work never hurt anyone.

CHICKLET: You're still young. Haven't you ever thought of remarrying?

MRS. FORREST: Your father was the great love of my life. I've always regretted that he died before you were born, that you never knew him. He was quite a guy. A damn good provider. And, darling, to even think of another man would betray his memory.

CHICKLET: I really love you, but I don't think I'm pulling my weight around here. I've been thinking, there must be more chores for me to do, painting the inside of the trash cans, polishing the cactus plants.

MRS. FORREST: Chicklet, I smell a rat.

CHICKLET: I'll exterminate it.

MRS. FORREST: Chicklet, what's going on up there in the old attic? *(Indicating her brain)*

CHICKLET: Okay, Mom, cards on the table. I need twenty-five dollars to buy a surfboard.

MRS. FORREST: Out of the question.

CHICKLET: Mom, it's the chance of a lifetime. The great Kanaka has promised to teach me to surf.

MRS. FORREST: The great who?

CHICKLET: The great Kanaka, why he's practically as famous as the President of the United States.

MRS. FORREST: It's too dangerous.

CHICKLET: It's as safe as playing jacks. Please let me Mom. It'll be sheer heaven or months and months of stark solitude.

MRS. FORREST: I will not have my daughter cavorting with a band of derelict beach bums.

CHICKLET: They're great guys. You should see them shooting the curl. It's the ultimate. A gilt-edged guarantee for a summer of sheer happiness.

MRS. FORREST: Control yourself, Florence.

CHICKLET *(fiercely):* I will not control myself! I want a mother-fucking cocksucking surfboard!!!!

MRS. FORREST: I can see the effect those boys are having on you. I don't like it one bit. You will not see those boys ever again. Promise me that.

CHICKLET: I will not promise you.

MRS. FORREST: You're cold. This is what the male sex is going to do to us. It's going to tear us apart. You don't know how lucky you are being a virgin, pure and chaste.

CHICKLET: But someday I do want to marry and then I suppose I'd have to . . .

MRS. FORREST: Do what? Have sexual intercourse. I know how they paint it so beautifully in the movies. A man and a woman locked in embrace, soft lighting, a pitcher of Manhattans, Rachmaninoff in the background. Well, my girl, let me tell you that is not how it is. You don't know how repugnant it is having a sweaty man's thing poking at you. *(She jabs her finger into* CHICKLET*)* Do you like that?

CHICKLET: Stop, you're hurting me.

MRS. FORREST: That's nothing compared to when they poke you down there.

CHICKLET: I don't believe you.

MRS. FORREST: Florence!

CHICKLET: I don't believe you. Sexual relations between a man and a woman in love is a beautiful and sacred thing. You're wrong, Mother, horribly wrong.

MRS. FORREST: The male body is coarse and ugly.

CHICKLET: Some men are beautiful.

MRS. FORREST *(in a demonic rage):* You think men are beautiful. Well, take a look at this, Missy. *(She pulls from her cleavage a jock strap)* For years I've kept this, anticipating this very moment. Do you know what this is?

CHICKLET: No.

MRS. FORREST: It's a peter belt. This is the pouch that holds their swollen genitalia. Isn't this beautiful? Isn't this romantic? *(She slaps* CHICKLET *with the jock strap repeatedly)*

CHICKLET: Stop, stop.

MRS. FORREST *(throws the jock strap at* CHICKLET): You are a very foolish girl. And to think I spent long hours toiling over that veal scallopini. (MRS. FORREST *exits.* CHICKLET *stares at the jock strap and whimpers)*

CHICKLET: I'm sorry, Mommy, I'm sorry. *(Starts growling and making animal noises. In baby talk)* She can't treat me this way. She's so mean and I'm too little to fight back . . . I'm so angry . . . I'm so angry! I'm . . . I'm *(She bursts into demonic laughter. As* ANN BOWMAN) I'm alive! I'm alive! Ann Bowman lives!!!!

(Blackout.)

Scene Three

(BERDINE *is in her pajamas writing in her diary*)

BERDINE: Dear Diary: Last night Chicklet showed up at my house with a real bee in her bonnet. She is determined to buy a surfboard. Her Mom said nix. Boy, parents can be grumps. Anyways, it's a good thing I won that prize money for my essay on Kierkegaard, Kant and Buber. I handed it right over. Chicklet Forrest is my best friend in the whole stratosphere. I've never told this to anyone, not even you, dear diary, but sometimes I catch her talking to herself in this weird sort of voice. I suppose some people would say she's kind of a burn-out, but you see, Chicklet is a very creative person and sometimes her imagination just sort of goes blotto, but in a noodly sort of way, not a complete geek-out, but just a fizzle in her research center. Sorry, that's teenage talk. Well, time to sign off, your ever faithful correspondent, Berdine.

(Blackout.)

Scene Four

The beach. YO YO *and* PROVOLONEY *enter talking.*

YO YO: I got my menu for the luau all made up. What do you think of marinated alligator tips? You can buy 'em frozen at Ralph's. And I thought lots of finger food, but no dips. I am so tired of dips.

PROVOLONEY: Yo Yo, would you stop with the food for a minute.

YO YO: But, Provoloney, the luau is only three weeks away.

PROVOLONEY: Do you realize how much of your life is obsessed with trivia? Finger food, dips. It really upsets me how little scope you have.

YO YO: What are you talking about? I've got scope. *(Switching the subject)* What do you want to do with your hair for the luau?

PROVOLONEY *(he screams):* See what I mean? Trivia! All this talk about recipes and hairstyles. People are gonna think you're kind of, you know, *(makes a limp wrist)* that way.

YO YO: Let 'em try. I'll bash their nuts in.

PROVOLONEY *(trying to talk sensibly):* Yo Yo, do you ever think about the future?

YO YO: Yeah, that's why I'm asking you about the alligator tips.

PROVOLONEY: The far future. You're not going to be young forever. We need to plan ahead.

YO YO: This was such a beautiful day. You're making me so depressed.

PROVOLONEY *(very upbeat):* Don't be depressed, kid. Stick with me and you'll never be sorry.

(STAR CAT *enters)*

STAR CAT: Hey guys, any of you seen Kanaka?

(KANAKA *and* CHICKLET *enter)*

KANAKA: Gentlemen, the time has come for me to introduce you to the new Empress of the Seven Seas. Queen Chicklet is going to join us on the water today.

PROVOLONEY: This little twirp working our waves, give me a break.

CHICKLET: I'm not a twirp.

YO YO: Stick to the bathtub, baby, leave the Pacific to the big boys.

STAR CAT: We're too busy to be changing your diapers.

CHICKLET: You think you know everything, you stuck up prune face pickle eater.

KANAKA: You ready for a ride, Chickerino?

CHICKLET: Kanaka, these fins are ready to hit the foam. What do you say?

KANAKA: I say, "Everybody, grab your surfboards and charge!" *(They all hoot and holler. Lights black out and then come back on and we see* CHICKLET *and the boys riding the high waves, laughing and screaming with joy and excitement. Blackout. When the lights come up, they are carrying* CHICKLET *on their shoulders, shouting "Hip hip hooray")* What did I tell you, ain't she something else?

YO YO *(making a big formal bow and kissing her hand):* I bow before the Queen Chicklet.

CHICKLET: Aw, knock it off.

PROVOLONEY: Welcome to the club. What do you say we make her our new mascot?

YO YO: Great.

STAR CAT: You know something, I am a stuck up prune face pickle eater. *(He gives* CHICKLET *a big hug and they embrace, a bit too long. Everyone's cheers turn to "Ohhhhhh," and they are embarrassed)* And I'll tell you what, I'll even teach you how to surf standing on your head.

CHICKLET *(thrilled):* You would? Really? Just the two of us?

YO YO *(imitating her):* Really? Just the two of us? *(All the guys giggle)*

CHICKLET *(embarrassed):* Well, I'd need to concentrate. I can't learn anything with you jokers around.

STAR CAT: Sure, kid, just the two of us.

PROVOLONEY *(acting silly):* Can we come, too?

YO YO: Please, please, pretty please. (CHICKLET *chases them around)*

CHICKLET: Oh gosh, this is the way I like it, just kids, horsing around, having picnics.

PROVOLONEY: We need to give her an initiation.

STAR CAT: And how.

CHICKLET: Oh, no you don't.

PROVOLONEY: Yo Yo, give her the Chinese tickle torture.

(They grab her and YO YO *pushes his head into her stomach tickling her with his hair, she screams.* MARVEL ANN *enters)*

MARVEL ANN: Star Cat. *(They drop* CHICKLET*)*

STAR CAT: Hey there, Marvel Ann.

STAR CAT *(she wraps herself around him):* What's all the brouhaha?

KANAKA: The Chicklet turned out to be a first class surfer.

YO YO: The best.

MARVEL ANN: How marvelous for you. I wish you every . . . every.

CHICKLET: You should try surfing, Marvel Ann, it's great for anyone with a weight problem.

MARVEL ANN: I get my exercise indoors. Star Cat, wait 'til you see the dress I bought to wear to the luau. It's very . . . very.

CHICKLET: What luau?

MARVEL ANN: Haven't you naughty boys told Chicklet about the luau? It's just the biggest event of the whole summer.

CHICKLET: You douche bags, why have you been holding out on me?

KANAKA: You're just not the luau type, baby.

PROVOLONEY: It's a wild night.

YO YO: Practically an orgy.

CHICKLET: I want to go.

MARVEL ANN: Besides you'll need an escort and I've already nabbed the cutest boy in town. *(Flirts with an uncomfortable* STAR CAT. *She strokes his hair)*

STAR CAT: Ow, you're pulling my hair.

MARVEL ANN: You promised you'd go to the pier with me today. I'm in the mood for a nice big banana split. Doesn't that sound tasty?

STAR CAT: Very, very. See you guys later. *(They exit)*

CHICKLET: You all think you're real clever not telling me about the luau, but I'm going and I'm going to make a splash like you've never seen.

(The incredibly glamourous movie star, BETTINA BARNES, *enters in a big hat and dark glasses. The boys stare at her transfixed as she unfolds her blanket and sits on the beach)*

YO YO: Zowie!

PROVOLONEY: Hot dog!

KANAKA: Let's check out her I.D. *(They approach her)*

CHICKLET: Hey guys, don't bother with her.

KANAKA *(to* BETTINA*)*: And then the Papa Bear said, "Who's been sleeping in my sandbox?"

BETTINA *(surprised, lowers her sunglasses):* Pardon me?

KANAKA: What brings you here to grace our turf?

BETTINA *(breathily innocent):* Am I trespassing? I had no idea.

PROVOLONEY: You look real familiar. Do you know Lenny Pinkowitz?

BETTINA *(alarmed):* Is he a shutterbug?

CHICKLET: Hey guys, come on.

YO YO: Can we ask you your name?

BETTINA: I'm afraid I can't answer that.

CHICKLET: Are you incognito?

BETTINA *(not comprehending):* No, I'm German-Irish.

KANAKA: Are there people after you?

BETTINA: I have a whole motion picture studio after me and the entire press corp. Haven't you read the newspapers? I'm Bettina Barnes. *(Gasps)* I shouldn't have told you.

CHICKLET: Bettina Barnes, the movie star.

BETTINA: Actress.

CHICKLET: You disappeared from the set of your new movie. The police think you've been kidnapped.

BETTINA: I was never kidnapped. I ran away.

PROVOLONEY: Why would you run away from a movie?

BETTINA: You don't know what it's like being exploited by those lousy flesh peddlers and power brokers. Everyone wanting a little piece. I'm not a pepperoni.

KANAKA: I saw you in that movie, "Sex Kittens Go To Outer Space."

BETTINA: That was a good film. The director had a vision, but then I had to do the four sequels. *Quel* trash. I couldn't go on. They have no respect for the rights of the individual.

YO YO: We'll respect you.

BETTINA *(touched):* Would you really? Isn't that what all human beings desire, respect? That's why I'm on the lam, to get me some.

CHICKLET: Where are you going to go?

BETTINA: New York. I've been accepted to study with Lee Strasberg. But first I thought I'd hide out here to get some rest and relaxation. I've rented that beach house over there. I signed the lease under my real name, Frieda Deefendorfer. You won't squeal on me, will you? *(The boys all promise they won't)* You're so sweet. You can be kind of like my brothers. *(To CHICKLET)* And you, you're perky. With a new hairstyle and the right makeup, you could be almost pretty.

(BERDINE *enters*)

BERDINE: Chicklet! There you are. I thought I'd find you here. You were supposed to meet me at the malt shop. I was waiting there over an hour when . . . *(She sees* BETTINA *and screams)* Bettina Barnes! *(The boys grab her and hold her mouth closed)*

CHICKLET: She's incognito.

BERDINE: Bettina Barnes. In person. You have the most beautiful eyelashes I've ever seen on any mammal.

BETTINA: You're very kind.

BERDINE: I loved you in "The Pizza Waitress with Three Heads." You were so real. When they trapped you on top of the pizzeria, you made me feel what it's like to have three heads and be shot in each one of them.

BETTINA *(intensely):* Did I really?

BERDINE: Oh yes, Miss Barnes.

BETTINA *(tenderly):* Call me Miss B. I know I could be a great actress if I found the right vehicle.

PROVOLONEY: She needs wheels.

YO YO: The lady needs wheels.

KANAKA: We'll get you a car.

BERDINE: No, she means she needs a great role that will reveal the many facets of her kaleidoscopic persona.

BETTINA *(confused):* What did she say?

BERDINE: Sometimes even the great don't understand their own power. You are more than a mere sex kitten. You are the feminine embodiment of the Nietzschian superman. Ever striving, striking a blow for the truth in the eternal battle of the sexes. Onward, Bettina! "And whatever will break on our truths, let it break! Many a house hath yet to be built." Thus spake Zarathustra.

BETTINA: That's what I've been telling my agents for months. You're smart. What's your name?

BERDINE: Berdine.

BETTINA: I desperately need a secretary slash companion slash masseuse. How would you like a job for the summer?

BERDINE: I don't know, Miss B. I've got a big reading list to get through. And I'm still not finished with "The Idiot."

BETTINA *(with great sympathy):* You've got man trouble?

PROVOLONEY: Hey guys, let's invite Miss Barnes to the luau.

BERDINE: What luau?

KANAKA: The first full moon of the summer, we have a luau slash barbecue. It's a night no one ever forgets.

BERDINE *(sarcastically):* Gee, thanks Chicklet for inviting me.

CHICKLET: I just heard about it.

BERDINE: Like hey I really believe that.

CHICKLET: It's the truth.

BERDINE: The truth is that we're not connecting at all anymore.

CHICKLET: What are you talking about?

BERDINE: Let me spell it out for you then. In the past few weeks, you never return my phone calls, you've cancelled out of the last five times we're supposed to get together and today you stood me up at Augie's malt shop. I don't think you want to be best friends anymore.

CHICKLET: I'm sorry, I just . . .

BERDINE *(holding back tears):* Everyone said we were too close. I never thought this could happen. Not to us.

BETTINA: Please don't argue on my account.

CHICKLET: Don't cry. Look, let's talk about this in private. How about meeting me at Augie's tomorrow?

BERDINE: So you can stand me up again? No, thank you. Chicklet, my closing remarks to you are these. I hope you enjoy all your new hipster friends cause you just lost your best and oldest one. Miss Barnes, I've reconsidered and I'd love to be your secretary. When do I start?

BETTINA: Pronto. We're going to have a great time. *(Takes her arm)* I'm going to let you in on all my innermost secrets. Let's go back to my bungalow and have lunch. You do know how to make Crab Louis, don't you?

BERDINE: I don't think so.

BETTINA: No sweat. We'll have peanut butter and jelly . . . *(as an afterthought)* on toast points.

PROVOLONEY: Think about the luau.

KANAKA: Think about me.

BETTINA *(seductively):* How could I forget you.

YO YO *(extends his hand to* BETTINA *to shake hands):* It's been great meeting you.

BETTINA (*she turns to* YO YO *and takes his hand*): My, what great big hands you have.

YO YO (*leering*): You know what they say about big hands and big feet.

BETTINA (*studying his hand intently*): Yes, most interesting.

CHICKLET: Are you a palmist or something?

BETTINA: No, nothing like that. I just have these incredible instincts about people. I seem to know how they tick.

YO YO: So what do you see?

BETTINA: I bet you're very good with hair.

YO YO: You mean running my fingers through it.

BETTINA: No, I mean setting it.

YO YO (*upset at the suggestion he's a fag*): Hey, wait just a minute . . .

BETTINA (*very soothing and gentle*): That's nothing to be ashamed of. It's a special gift. (*The other guys snicker*) I've got a slew of wigs with me. Let's go to my bungalow, lock the door and play beauty salon.

PROVOLONEY (*acting sexy*): Can I come too? I'd love to lock the door and play with you.

BETTINA: Hey, Berdine, as a great philosopher once said "the more the merrier." Let's go!

YO YO: Yeah, go, go, go. (BETTINA *exits followed by* YO YO, PROVOLONEY *and* BERDINE. KANAKA *pulls* CHICKLET *back*)

KANAKA: Hey, Chicklet.

CHICKLET: Don't you want to go to Bettina's?

KANAKA: Nah, it's kids stuff to be impressed with her. *(Checks to see if they are alone)*

CHICKLET: Who are you looking for?

KANAKA: I want to make sure we're alone. Uh, it's Yo Yo's birthday coming up and . . .

CHICKLET: I thought he said it was . . .

KANAKA: No, it's real soon and I thought you could help me make him a present.

CHICKLET: Like what?

KANAKA: A kite. He's flipped over kites. What do you think of that?

CHICKLET: A kite. That's okay.

KANAKA: Kites. He becomes like a different person when he's flying a kite.

CHICKLET: I never made one before but . . .

KANAKA *(to himself)*: What were we talking about? Do you see that fish jumping out of the water?

CHICKLET: No, where?

KANAKA: I'm crazy for fish, aren't you?

CHICKLET *(shrugs)*: Feh. Kanaka, are you all right?

KANAKA *(giving up)*: No, I must be out of my mind. Forget it. Geez, I'm embarrassed. Is my face red? *(When CHICKLET hears red, she laughs wildly and turns into ANN BOWMAN)*

KANAKA *(elated):* It was a red kite!

CHICKLET *(as* ANN BOWMAN*):* It most certainly was, darling. As red as your ass when I finish spanking you.

KANAKA: Oh yes, Mistress Ann. I've been a bad boy. I need a spanking.

CHICKLET: I've got you under my spell. You would do anything I asked. *(She turns into* TYLENE, *a black checkout girl)* But if she asked me to work overtime at that Safeway, she be out of her mind.

KANAKA: Ann?

CHICKLET: Who you be calling Ann, my name is Tylene. Tylene Carmichael Carmel.

KANAKA: What?

CHICKLET: I be working at the checkout, it goin' on four-thirty and I'm fixin' to leave. My boyfriend, he's taking me to see Chubby Checker.

KANAKA: Ann, come back, Ann, are you there?

CHICKLET: Would you let me finish? What I am saying is my supervisor, Miss Feeley, she asks me to work overtime. She thinks she so cool, she . . .

KANAKA *(shakes her):* Stop it. Bring Ann back!

CHICKLET *(indicates a switchblade's in her pocket):* Back off! I cut you. I cut you. I got me a blade. I cut you.

KANAKA *(terrified):* That's cool. That's cool.

CHICKLET: No way no white son of a bitch be grabbin at me. No way, no way . . . *(Returns as* ANN*)* No way you can escape my domination. The world has tried to suppress me, to deny my very existence but I have risen like a phoenix to claim my birthright.

KANAKA: What's that?

CHICKLET: World domination. Ann Bowman, Dominatrix Empress of the planet Earth. Has a catchy ring, don't you think?

KANAKA: Yes, Mistress Ann.

CHICKLET: I wonder if your little friends might make excellent slaves. We must catch them in butterfly nets and put them in cages. Once their spirit is broken, they shall learn to serve their Mistress Ann.

KANAKA: Cages. But won't they suspect you're up to no good?

CHICKLET: I am not only a first class general. I am also a brilliant actress. I will pose as dear little Chicklet and infiltrate the teen set.

KANAKA: Look, I think I've gotten in over my head. I can't do something like this.

CHICKLET *(grabbing him):* You deny me! No one denies me, darling. You need what only I can offer. Face it, you're weak, you're a pushover for me. You sing to the coppers and I'll finger you as the fall guy. You made me lose my temper. It's time for fun and games. Shall we proceed to your place? Kanaka, move it! *(She throws her head back and laughs. They exit. Blackout.)*

Scene Five

The beach. PROVOLONEY *and* YO YO *enter.*

YO YO: I don't know, Provoloney, it sounds too easy.

PROVOLONEY: I tell you, the ideas that make millions are deceptively simple. Bettina Barnes is on the lookout for a movie that will win her an Oscar. We've got to find it for her.

YO YO: But that means writing and I'm not so good with sentences.

PROVOLONEY: In Hollywood, only flunkies do any writing. The smart guys write treatments. The studio pays big money just for ideas. We come up with a great notion for a flick and we can rake in the moola without putting in a comma.

YO YO: You have any ideas?

PROVOLONEY: My brain's bursting with them. Westerns, sci-fi, musicals.

YO YO: Well, I think . . .

PROVOLONEY: Quiet on the set. I need inspiration. I need a concept.

YO YO: I think Bettina should play the richest woman in the world.

PROVOLONEY *(his eyes closed):* Yeah, my mind's working now. Go on.

YO YO: Her old man wants her to marry this prince, but he's kind of a drip so she ankles out of Philly and heads westward to Malibu.

PROVOLONEY: It's all coming to me. I'm cookin'. Go on.

YO YO: She's got so much cash that she buys the whole beach. There's this real hot surf bum who lives there and he don't like the idea of being evicted. They decide to smoke the peace pipe and the stud offers to teach her to scuba dive.

PROVOLONEY: This is great. I can see the whole thing. A billboard fifty feet high. Bettina Barnes in a wet suit.

YO YO: I see this real big scene when they first dive underwater. (YO YO *mimes going underwater)*

PROVOLONEY *(he dives too):* They swim past picturesque coral reefs and dolphins.

YO YO: And they bump into each other. *(They mime all the next activity)*

PROVOLONEY: And they get their feet caught in some seaweed . . . and their bodies are locked into each other.

YO YO: They can't get out?

PROVOLONEY *(transfixed):* Uh uh. Their eyes meet. Every night he's dreamt of her long flowing hair, her ivory skin, her biceps.

YO YO: She feels powerless to resist his raw brute strength. Is this where they kiss for the first time?

PROVOLONEY: They've always wanted to, but they were too scared.

YO YO: I guess underwater it doesn't matter much.

PROVOLONEY: I guess not.

(They slowly kiss. Cannons go off. Bells ring. The 1812 Overture is played. They break apart)

PROVOLONEY *(scared):* Uh, Yo Yo, I better write this down before I forget it.

YO YO *(thrilled):* I won't forget it.

PROVOLONEY *(embarrassed and remorseful):* I met this lady who works in the library. She said she'd teach me how to use her typewriter.

YO YO: That's good.

PROVOLONEY: Yeah. Maybe afterwards, I'll . . . I'll ball her. (PROVOLONEY *exits. Blackout.)*

Scene Six

The beach beyond BETTINA*'s house.* BERDINE *is writing in her diary.*

BERDINE: Dear Diary: Gear up for another helping of Berdine's flaming self pity. I miss Chicklet so much. Ever since she got that darn surfboard, nothing's been the same. I wish I'd never given her that money. A girl's best friend is something very special. And Chicklet's more than just my best friend. It's like we're one person. I know that sounds kooky, but it's true. Oh, life is but a meaningless charade, death the ultimate absurdity. I am living proof of Sartre's existential concept of nausea. Gosh, I wish I had a Tums. Of course, I've been very busy working for Miss Barnes. She's a nice lady, but very complicated. (BETTINA *enters stretching*) Good morning, Miss B!

BETTINA: What a splendiforous morning. I can't tell you how grand it feels to be away from that salacious Hollywood rat race. I was so tense. You can't imagine the hubbub in my lower lumbar region.

BERDINE: Well, this week has done wonders for you. You look like a completely different person.

BETTINA *(suspicious and paranoid):* Who? What are her measurements?

BERDINE: No, what I meant was . . . oh . . . *(Sees telegram in her hand)* Oh! Miss Barnes, that telegram arrived that you were waiting for.

BETTINA *(excited):* Oh wow, I'm scared to open it. It's from the studio. I've asked them to release me from my contract. *(Opens it)* I'm too scared to read it. It's awful being this vulnerable. *(To* BERDINE) You read it to me.

BERDINE *(reading):* Dear Bettina, up yours, stop, with turpentine, stop. New picture "Sex Kittens Go Bossa Nova" starts lensing September first. Be there or expect legal action. Stop. Love Sid Rosen. *(Stops reading)* Oh Bettina, I'm so sorry. You poor little thing.

BETTINA *(tough as nails and in a low rough voice):* That cheap son of a bitch can't do this to me. He slaps me with a subpoena and I'll have his balls on a plate.

BERDINE *(shocked):* Bettina.

BETTINA *(pacing, furious):* After all the money I made for those bastards. They can't do this to me. I'm Bettina Barnes. I'm no flash in the pan that'll take any piece of crap. I'm playing hard ball, baby.

BERDINE: Have you read the script? Maybe it's not bad.

BETTINA: Not bad! Lassie could fart out a better script.

(YO YO *and* PROVOLONEY *enter.* PROVOLONEY *is tricked up in his notion of a Hollywood movie mogul)*

PROVOLONEY: Hey there, Miss Barnes, I hear you got some work you'd like us to do.

BETTINA *(soft and vulnerable):* Oh, yeah, something. I needed something done. I'm so forgetful. *(Remembers)* Oh, yes. Last night I was sleepwalking and I suddenly woke up and discovered this adorable little garden in my backyard. During the last storm, all the little trees and shrubbery must have broken and it's a dreadful mess. Could you clear it up for me? And then we can have swell parties. I make delicious jalapeno pancakes.

YO YO: Sure thing. We'll clean it up.

PROVOLONEY *(nervously):* Excuse me Miss Barnes, do you think I could talk to you for a moment?

BETTINA: But of course.

PROVOLONEY *(with an air of bravado):* I never told you this before, but this surf bum business is just a facade, I'm really a screenwriter.

BERDINE: You're what?

YO YO: He's a screenwriter.

PROVOLONEY: Written tons of stuff, T.V., radio. I've got a development deal going for me at Columbia. Meeting you yesterday gave me the inspiration for a new picture. A big picture, cinemascope, 3-D, smell-o-vision.

BETTINA *(touched):* Really, I inspired you?

PROVOLONEY: You certainly did. It's just a treatment, really, an idea.

YO YO: But it's a great one.

BETTINA: I love a man with a big idea.

PROVOLONEY: Columbia's been putting the screws on me to make it with Kim.

BETTINA *(very impressed):* You know Kim Novak?

PROVOLONEY: Great gal, but dead eyes, blank, an empty screen. This idea . . .

BETTINA: Oh, tell me all about it.

PROVOLONEY: The setting: Malibu Beach. I see you as the daughter of a shipping tycoon. You . . .

BERDINE: . . . leave finishing school and meet a handsome surf bum who teaches you how to scuba dive. "The Girl From Rock n' Roll Beach," starring Mamie Van Doren, Allied Artists, 1960, Albert Zugsmith, producer.

PROVOLONEY: Yeah, well, it's a lot like that, only better. You can have the whole *megillah* for two thousand dollars.

BETTINA: Two thousand dollars. It sounds most intriguing, but I think for my first independent feature, I should play a typical girl of today, someone who the audience can identify with and yet a girl with a personal problem, like psoriasis. However, maybe we can develop this further.

PROVOLONEY: Bettina baby, I don't want to pressure you but . . .

BETTINA *(looks offstage):* Oh, look, there's your little friend, Chicklet. I don't know, there's something kind of funny about her.

(CHICKLET *enters with a wild red feather boa, smoking out of a long cigarette holder)*

CHICKLET *(in* ANN BOWMAN's *voice):* Berdine darling! It's been eons since we last met.

BERDINE *(shocked):* Chicklet?

CHICKLET: Miss Barnes, a delight as always. *(To the boys)* Hello, boys. *(They all say "Hi" in a dazed manner)* I do hope these boys have been showing you a good time. They taught me how to surf and now I'm positively addicted to shooting the curl, as they say.

BETTINA: They're helping me fix up my backyard.

CHICKLET: How utterly fab. Boys, I have a little job for you.

YO YO: Chicklet, are you feeling all right?

CHICKLET: Just swellsville. I'd like to have a cage built.

PROVOLONEY: A bird cage?

CHICKLET: No, something suitable for a bigger animal, or animals.

BERDINE: Chicklet, what are you talking about?

CHICKLET *(becomes herself):* Berdine. Where am I? *(Sees the boa and cigarette holder)* What's all this?

BERDINE: You tell me.

CHICKLET *(at a loss):* Ohhh, I found it in the garbage outside the Club Transvestite. *(She laughs hysterically, but no one else does)* Eek.

PROVOLONEY: You wanted us to build you a cage.

CHICKLET: A cage? Don't be a doofus . . . Anyways, now that I am here . . . Berdine, I feel awful for the way I've been treating you. I don't know what could possess me being so rude like that. You should just belt me. Go on and belt me.

BERDINE: I couldn't.

CHICKLET: Really. You're like my . . . How do I . . .

BERDINE: I know. You are too.

CHICKLET: But more than that. We've always . . .

BERDINE: That's true. But still sometimes . . .

CHICKLET: Oh, but we . . .

BERDINE: Yeah, but I wouldn't want . . .

CHICKLET: You don't really want . . .

BERDINE: I just don't . . .

CHICKLET: Trust me. C'mon. Please Berdine, please go on being my best friend for a zillion more years. What do you say?

BERDINE: For a zillion trillion more years. To infinity. *(They hug)*

CHICKLET: Will you be my escort to the luau?

BERDINE: You don't think I'm too much of a nerd-brain?

CHICKLET: Of course not.

PROVOLONEY: What are you two going to do for the talent show?

CHICKLET: What talent show?

YO YO: That's part of the tradition. Everyone's gotta get up and do an act. I'm doing my Jane Russell imitation. *(Pulls his shirt out like bosoms)* Boom titty boom.

BERDINE: I know. Remember that act we did for the Kiwanis Club Variety Night? The costume is in my attic.

CHICKLET: You got yourself a partner. *(They shake)*

BETTINA: I'm glad you patched things up. I'm so in awe of friendship. I mean, never having any. We better get started on the garden before it gets dark. Come on, kids.

(All the kids including CHICKLET and BERDINE exit laughing and singing. STAR CAT and MARVEL ANN stroll on)

MARVEL ANN: Star Cat, you mean little devil, I was up all night thinking about you.

STAR CAT *(excited):* You were?

MARVEL ANN: Uh huh. Couldn't sleep a wink. You wanna know what I was thinking?

STAR CAT: Empty that beautiful head of yours.

MARVEL ANN: I was thinking that you and I are going to be united as one forever.

STAR CAT *(nervously):* Gee, Marvel Ann, are you sure I'm good enough for you? I wouldn't want you to settle.

MARVEL ANN: Settle? You're the dreamboat of all time, generous, always thinking of others, sensitive.

STAR CAT: Aw, I'm just a good for nothing surf bum.

MARVEL ANN: That's not true. You're just riddled with greatness. I look in your eyes and honestly, I see dollar signs.

STAR CAT: You don't understand. I'm rejecting those false values. I refuse to worship the golden calf.

MARVEL ANN *(petulant but still pleasant):* You don't know what you want. I think it's a horrid shame that you're throwing away a great future as a psychiatrist. All your wonderful compassion going to waste. (STAR CAT *tries to interject)* Oh, I know what you're going to say, "I just want a little shack by the water." Well, you can't expect me to live like that. Imagine me serving my friends Steak Diane Flambé in a lean-to. (STAR CAT *tries to interject)* Don't say a word, I know what you're thinking, "Marvel Ann is such a lovely person, in time she'd grow used to such a life." *(With growing emotion and intensity)* Well, I'd be humiliated. Oh, I can read you like the funny papers. *(With growing fury)* You think I'm so head over heels in love with you, I'll accept whatever crumbs you have to offer. Well, no siree Bob, I am hardly a desperate female. Ohhh, look at that awful expression in your eyes. I bet you think you don't even have to marry me, that I'd shack up with you like a common whore. Now you've really done it. I am livid. How could you think of such filth! You are a selfish, egocentric creep and my advice to you is to straighten up, buckle down and apply yourself like any other decent, normal Presbyterian!!

(She stalks off in a fury. CHICKLET *enters)*

STAR CAT *(angrily):* Hey, what are you doing here?

CHICKLET: I didn't know you owned this beach. I don't see your initials carved into the ocean.

STAR CAT: Sorry. I didn't mean to bark at you.

CHICKLET *(sympathetically):* Girl trouble?

STAR CAT: Yeah, that dame wants to put a ball and chain around my neck.

CHICKLET: Well, don't you dare let her. I think it's swell the way you guys live.

STAR CAT: You do?

CHICKLET: Sure. Flying about as free as a gull, never having a care in the world.

STAR CAT: You're on my beam. Marvel Ann doesn't understand me at all. She thinks she can see through me like wax paper, but she's wrong. I'm an extremely complex person with deep rooted neuroses and anxieties. You wouldn't understand that, you're just a kid.

CHICKLET (offended): I am not just a kid. I'm capable of intensely passionate adult feelings. If you didn't have so much sea foam in your eyes, you'd notice I'm a budding young woman.

STAR CAT (amused): Honey, your buds have a long way to bloom.

CHICKLET: Evidently some people don't share that opinion.

STAR CAT: Like who?

CHICKLET: Oh, some people.

STAR CAT: Like nobody.

CHICKLET: Like Kanaka. He thinks I'm, how did he put it? I'm a luscious voluptuary.

STAR CAT: Liar. I know Kanaka. He could have any dame in Malibu.

CHICKLET: Well, he wants me.

STAR CAT: How do you know?

CHICKLET: It's one of those mystical things a woman feels instinctively in her soul.

STAR CAT: Get over it.

CHICKLET *(defensively):* He taught me how to surf, didn't he? And he tries to see me every day and he always makes sure we're completely alone. As a matter of fact, I'm headed over to Kanaka's shack right now, for an extremely intimate tête-a-tête.

STAR CAT: I don't believe it.

CHICKLET: *Chacon à son gout.* That means, each to his own, you dope. He thinks I'm special.

STAR CAT: I think you're trying to make me jealous. What a screwy kid you are. I bet you've got a great big fat crush on me.

CHICKLET *(blushing):* You've got a great big fat ego.

STAR CAT: Hey c'mon, let's call it a truce. I like you, kid. I do. And I think you're very special.

CHICKLET: Please don't patronize me.

STAR CAT *(turns her around and holds her chin):* You are special.

CHICKLET *(vulnerable):* I am?

STAR CAT: And cute.

CHICKLET: I am?

STAR CAT: You need somebody to protect you.

CHICKLET: Protect me from what?

STAR CAT *(friendly):* Oh, from big bad wolves. You could be a tasty morsel, to some wolf.

CHICKLET: What about to you?

STAR CAT: I suppose I could be dangerously tempted.

CHICKLET: Oh, Star Cat.

(STAR CAT opens his mouth to sing. We hear an obviously dubbed recording of a teen idol singing the "Chicklet Theme Song." Suddenly, the record gets stuck, and we hear the needle scratch across the record. There is an uncomfortable silence)

STAR CAT: I guess I'll have to tell you how I feel. You're a one of a kind girl, Chicklet, like no one I've ever met.

CHICKLET: What about Marvel Ann? Is she one of a kind too?

STAR CAT *(smiles, embarrassed):* Well . . .

CHICKLET: Star Cat, what do boys do when they're alone with a girl?

STAR CAT: You can't ask me such a question.

CHICKLET: Why not? I want to know.

STAR CAT: They neck. I don't know.

CHICKLET: What do you do with Marvel Ann?

STAR CAT: This is embarrassing, Chicklet.

CHICKLET: Tell me.

(Romantic music sneaks in through the end of the scene)

STAR CAT: She nestles real close to me.

CHICKLET (*cuddles next to him*): Kind of like this?

STAR CAT (*horny and nervous*): Yeah, sort of like that. I hold her in my arms. And she holds me back.

CHICKLET: Like this? And then what do you do?

STAR CAT: I kiss the back of her neck. I can't do this with you.

CHICKLET: Pretend I'm Marvel Ann. I need to know this sort of thing. For my own protection.

STAR CAT: I stroke her arm and she kisses my chest. (CHICKLET *kisses his chest*) And we can feel our hearts beating as one. We find ourselves swaying to the same personal rhythm.

CHICKLET: You take your clothes off, right?

STAR CAT (*lost in the moment*): Uh huh.

CHICKLET: You got your clothes off. Then what?

STAR CAT: I caress her smooth satiny flesh. It glistens in the moonlight. She gently touches my muscles with her fingertips. Our bodies seem to float to the ground. We're entwined. And then I slowly slide my penis into her vagina. Simultaneously, she licks her index finger and inserts it up my rectum as I pump my penis . . .

(*During this last graphic part,* CHICKLET *is horrified and at the end of his speech, she screams as if in a horror movie and runs away*)

STAR CAT (*shouting after her*): Chicklet, come back!

(*Blackout.*)

Scene Seven

Kanaka's shack. STAR CAT *enters.*

STAR CAT: Kanaka, where are you? You home?

(KANAKA *enters*)

KANAKA: Hey pal, what are you doing in my shack without an invite? I don't dig surprise visits.

STAR CAT: I'm looking for Chicklet.

KANAKA: She's not here, not yet.

STAR CAT: But she will be.

KANAKA: Yeah, and what's it to you? She's not your chick.

STAR CAT: And she shouldn't be yours either. She's only a kid.

KANAKA: That's all you know.

STAR CAT: If you've laid a finger on her . . .

KANAKA: Hey, cool out. You don't know the score. There is more to that Chicklet than meets the old eyeball. There's like two Chicklets in one, man.

STAR CAT: What are you talking about?

KANAKA: It's wild. She's like twins in one bod. One's an angel and the other's a she devil. She calls herself Ann Bowman and she's like a demon. And the weird thing is, I can turn her off and on like a flashlight.

STAR CAT: You're talking crazy.

KANAKA (desperate): Can I trust you, buddy? Will you swear by the code of the King of the Sea you won't tell anyone any of this?

STAR CAT: Yeah, I swear.

KANAKA: I got it heavy for Ann Bowman. She's like a drug running through my veins and I can't shake her. I'm even gonna let her shave me, man.

STAR CAT: You're not making any sense.

KANAKA: Nothing makes sense. But I need her. I need Mistress Ann.

STAR CAT: Get a hold of yourself.

KANAKA: She's power mad. She's plotting to take over the world. First Malibu and then Sacramento. She wants to set up concentration camps for her enemies and public executions and her own NBC variety series.

(CHICKLET *enters unseen by them*)

STAR CAT: If this is true, you've got to stop this!

KANAKA: I can't give her up. I'd kill for Ann Bowman.

CHICKLET: Who's Ann Bowman?

STAR CAT: Stay out of this.

KANAKA: Star Cat, I want you to meet a friend of mine. Hey, Chicklet, you remember that kite we saw, that . . .

STAR CAT: You son of a . . . (STAR CAT *tries to punch out* KANAKA. *They fight.* CHICKLET *tries to get between them. Suddenly they all start to move in slow motion and we see* CHICKLET *get in the way of* STAR CAT's *punch and slowly drift to the floor*) Chicklet, are you all right?

KANAKA: Now you've done it, man. (*They both hold her as she comes to*)

CHICKLET: What happened? Where am I?

KANAKA: In my beach shack.

(*There's wild knocking at the door*)

KANAKA: The door's open.

(MRS. FORREST *enters in a furious state*)

MRS. FORREST: Well, this is a pretty sight, I must say.

KANAKA: Who the hell are you?

CHICKLET: Mom, what are you doing here?

MRS. FORREST: Young lady, you are in big trouble.

STAR CAT: Mrs. Forrest, you don't understand.

MRS. FORREST: Indeed I do understand. I also know the penalty for seducing a minor. You and your buddy will be sitting in stir for quite a while.

CHICKLET: Mother, would you stop. Kanaka and Star Cat are my friends. There was nothing dirty involved.

MRS. FORREST: How dare you speak to me in that manner. I see now clearly the effect of a permissive childhood. All the gentle caring, the indulgences, the little treats. How wrong I was. Life will be quite different from now on. I am going to mete out a severe punishment for you, young lady, most severe indeed.

CHICKLET: Mother.

MRS. FORREST: Get in the car. (CHICKLET *exits. To the boys*) You two scum bags had better get yourselves a good mouthpiece, cause I'm gonna tear your peckers off in that courtroom. Good evening, gentlemen.

(Blackout.)

Scene Eight

BERDINE *is in her bedroom writing in her diary.*

BERDINE: Dear Diary: This entry is strictly confidential. Chicklet's Mom is on the warpath. She locked the Chicklet in her room and has refused her all visitors, yours truly included. Panicsville, here I come. The luau is tomorrow night! Chicklet and I simply have to be there. We've been rehearsing our Siamese twin act all week. It's gonna be the greatest thing ever. I swear, grownups think they can run the whole world. Like Nathan Hale or Lafayette Escadrille, there is only one person who refuses to bow down before tyranny, I Berdine! I'm marching over to Chicklet's right now and get her out of there. I defy you stars, nothing and I mean nothing is going to stop us from going to the luau.

(Blackout. Lights up. We are in CHICKLET's *bedroom.* CHICKLET *is bound and gagged. A T.V. tray with dinner is placed before her.* MRS. FORREST *enters with creepy serenity)*

MRS. FORREST: What a dinner. I'm so stuffed I can hardly move. I certainly enjoyed my T-bone steak, so bloody rare and juicy. *(Thoughtfully)* I may have overcooked the lima beans. Vegetables are delicate creatures. *(With vulnerable charm)* Still, I have to admit, it was delicious. *(Still lovely)* This meal could have been yours, Chicklet, if you hadn't chosen to disobey me. Do you finally see what I mean about making the right choices in life? It's a rough world, darling, with a lot of crummy people out there. You can't be impressed with them. *(With force)* Believe me, they stink! *(Back to her charming manner)* I'm afraid I still see defiance in your eyes. You have so much to learn. *(She touches the gag restraint. Jokes)* I bet you think I've taken this gag too far. *(Laughs at her joke)* That's funny. *(She gives the gag a tighter tug)* I think we'll keep this on a wee bit longer. *(She exits)*

(BERDINE *enters swinging in through the window on a rope made of bedsheets)*

BERDINE: Chicklet! What has she done to you? *(She tries to untie her)* You poor helpless thing. How did she do this? These must be army knots. Don't be mad, but I think our top priority should be your arms. I hope this experience won't make you bitter and pessimistic. Just hold on. I'm not saying you should be a grinning idiot, but as Schopenhauer says, "We should strive for a tragic optimism." (CHICKLET *grunts)* It's not easy, the greater the intelligence, the greater the capacity for suffering. (CHICKLET *grunts.* MRS. FORREST *enters unbeknownst to* BERDINE *whose back is to her.* CHICKLET *sees* MRS. FORREST *and grunts trying to warn* BERDINE) I can't get it. We'll have to get you out of here the way you are. Give a little hop. (BERDINE *turns around and sees* MRS. FORREST)

MRS. FORREST *(exuding charm):* Hello Berdine. How kind of you to visit us. I've made a terrific bunt cake. Care for a slice?

BERDINE *(totally freaked):* That's okay. My Mom made butterscotch pudding for dessert. I've really got to get along.

MRS. FORREST: Such a pity. I was hoping you'd watch "Bonanza" with us. Are you planning to take Chicklet with you?

BERDINE: Uh yes, actually. We've been rehearsing . . . I mean we've been working on a science project together. Mendel's theory of propagation and all that stuff.

MRS. FORREST: I'm afraid Mendel will have to propagate without the help of my Chicklet. She's been a naughty girl and naughtiness must be punished. Chicklet lied to me and more importantly she lied to herself. Berdine, you must be brutally honest with yourself, cruelly honest. Rip away the cobwebs of delusion. Dig and find the ugliness at the base of your soul, expose it to the light, examine it, let it wither, then kill it!!! Girl, know thyself! *(Trying to control her emotions)* It's the only way.

BERDINE *(caught up in the debate and forgetting* CHICKLET): Mrs. Forrest, I fervently disagree. (CHICKLET *grunts desperately)* One must seek self knowledge, but illusion is necessary to preserve a sense of innocence.

MRS. FORREST *(pulls* CHICKLET *to her):* None are innocent, all are guilty.

BERDINE *(realizes* MRS. FORREST *isn't on her wavelength):* Mrs. Forrest, you're a fascinating conversationalist, but I've really got to get Chicklet out of here.

MRS. FORREST *(forcefully):* Chicklet is grounded!

BERDINE: Get out of my way, Mrs. Forrest. I am rescuing Chicklet. You are not responsible for your actions.

MRS. FORREST: You take one more step and you'll be a nerd with no teeth.

BERDINE: To save Chicklet, I would gladly wear a complete bridge. (BERDINE *moves and* MRS. FORREST *grabs her. They wrestle to the ground and fight it out. Finally* BERDINE *gets the upper hand and sits on* MRS. FORREST's *chest, pinning her down)* Chicklet, run for it!

MRS. FORREST *(gasping):* Get off me, you big cow! (CHICKLET *with her feet bound slowly hops offstage while* BERDINE *talks to* MRS. FORREST)

BERDINE *(ties* MRS. FORREST *up with bedsheets):* I'm really sorry, Mrs. Forrest, for being so disrespectful. This is highly uncharacteristic behavior for me, but you know, lately I've been cramming myself with Sartrean existentialism so maybe I'm unduly influenced by his committment to extreme action. Gosh, this is deep.

(Blackout.)

Scene Nine

The luau. Lights up and PROVOLONEY, YO YO, KANAKA, BET-
TINA, NICKY *and* DEE DEE *are all having a wild time.* STAR CAT
enters.

STAR CAT: Marvel Ann, Marvel Ann! Has anybody seen Marvel
Ann?

EVERYONE: No!

NICKY: Hey cats, let's limbo!

*(They do a big limbo number and hoot it up. At the height of
the festivities,* MARVEL ANN *enters, her hair half shaved off.*
BETTINA *is the first to see her and screams)*

MARVEL ANN *(hysterical):* My hair! My hair! I'm gonna kill the
bastard who did this.

STAR CAT: Marvel Ann, what happened?

MARVEL ANN: I was lying on the beach with my eyes closed. Someone knocked me out. I woke up and the bastard was shaving my head. They'd already shaved my beaver.

PROVOLONEY: Couldn't you see who it was?

MARVEL ANN: No, they had glued stripper's pasties over my eyes. I'm so humiliated.

KANAKA *(in terror to* STAR CAT*)*: Ann Bowman strikes again.

BETTINA: Honey, in a few months you'll have a cute pixie. (MARVEL ANN *groans.* PROVOLONEY *jumps up trying to get everyone's attention)*

PROVOLONEY: Quiet, everybody. QUIET! *(Everyone settles down to watch the show)* Good evening and welcome to Provoloney's Pacific Follies. How is everybody out there? Ready for a great show? Let me hear you.

NICKY: Boo! Get on with the show. *(Everyone joins in booing)*

PROVOLONEY: I love these audiences, the greatest in the world. I tell you, coming over here tonight I couldn't help but be reminded of the story of the stewardess in from Cleveland. She arrives at . . .

NICKY: We heard that already. Bring on the girls. *(Everyone joins in)*

PROVOLONEY: Rough house. Okay, you want entertainment, I'll give you entertainment with a capital E. There's nothing I like better than discovering young talent. And I . . .

NICKY: Where did they discover you? Under a rock? Get on with it.

PROVOLONEY *(getting mad):* What I'm doing is laying the foundation for the evening at . . .

NICKY: You're laying an egg. *(Everyone laughs)*

PROVOLONEY: I've gotten big laughs from tougher crowds than you.

NICKY: Before or after you dropped your pants? *(Everyone laughs)*

PROVOLONEY *(furious):* That does it! I don't have to take this. Do your own stinkin' show. (STAR CAT *jumps up and soothes* PROVOLONEY's *ego)*

STAR CAT: Aw, c'mon, he's just joshing you. You're doing great. Go on. Guys, give him some support. *(They applaud)*

PROVOLONEY: Well, if you insist. Without further ado *(He gives* NICKY *a dirty look)* please give a warm hand to a sister act that ends all sister acts. Straight from exotic Siam, the spectacular, the inseparable, Hester and Esther. Take it away, girls.

(CHICKLET *and* BERDINE *enter in a wild red siamese twin costume joined at the hip)*

CHICKLET: My name is Esther.

BERDINE: My name is Hester.

BERDINE and CHICKLET *(in unison):*
Life ain't always a pip
when you're joined at the hip.

If just a small bump
does strange things to your rump,

and a hot stripper's grind
really aches your behind,

but enuf of this kvetching,
we still look most fetching,

so vo de oh do,
let's get on with the show.

(CHICKLET *and* BERDINE *begin singing a song such as "The Lady in Red."* * *In the middle of the song,* CHICKLET *begins talking to herself.* BERDINE *continues to sing)*

CHICKLET: Red . . . red . . . red dress. *(Mutters)* Take that off. You look like a whore. Take that dress off. *(Cries like a baby)* I'm angry. I'm angry. I don't like this. I can't move. Get me out. (BERDINE *continues to sing nervously.* CHICKLET *makes animal sounds)*

BERDINE: Chicklet, please. "The Lady in Red," the fellas are crazy about the . . .

CHICKLET *(muttering):* Crazy, crazy, the fellas are crazy . . . about ME! Me, Ann Bowman, live, onstage! *(Laughs raucously)* At last, in the spotlight.

BERDINE *(nervously improvising):* Now Chicklet's going to do some impersonations for you. Who are you doing, Chicklet?

CHICKLET *(as* ANN*):* Get your hands off me, you blithering bull dyke.

BETTINA: What's going on?

CHICKLET *(as* ANN*):* Silence! Now that I have your attention, I'd like to sing my song, my SOLO! *(Crooning)* More than the greatest love the world has known . . . *(As a little girl)* Stop, I don't like your singing, you scare me. *(As* ANN*)* Shut up, you little bitch! *(As* TYLENE*)* Don't you be talking to that

* Note: Permission to produce PSYCHO BEACH PARTY does not *include permission to use this song. Producers are hereby cautioned that they must procure such permission from the copyright owner, Warner Bros., Inc., 9000 Sunset Blvd., Los Angeles, CA 90069.*

chile like that. *(As* ANN) Do not underestimate my fury, Tylene. *(As* TYLENE) I ain't scared of you, mother. *(As* DR. ROSE MAYER) Excuse me, if I may interject. This is Dr. Rose Mayer speaking. If you have a personal grievance, by all means you are entitled to a fair hearing, but let us not air out our dirty laundry in public. *(As* ANN) Butt out, you blabbering battleax. *(As* DR. ROSE MAYER) Once more I must interject. Ann, the question I ask of you is why? Why cause all this *tsouris,* this unhappiness. *(As* ANN) Enough! You insolent fools! I am taking over Chicklet's mind once and for all. Chicklet is officially dead!

BERDINE: Stop it, stop it!

CHICKLET *(as* ANN): I warned you not to touch me. *(She starts to strangle* BERDINE. STAR CAT *and* KANAKA *try to separate them.* CHICKLET *pulls out a straight razor and the chase is on.* CHICKLET *is on the rampage, chasing all the kids, dragging* BERDINE *behind her)* It's a shave and a haircut for all of you. How about white sidewalls, honey. *(She moves toward* BETTINA) I'll get you anyway, Peewee.

BETTINA *(holding her ponytail):* It's a fake! It's a switch! Help! Help! (STAR CAT *and* KANAKA *subdue* CHICKLET. *They pin her arms back and grab the razor.* BERDINE *is in hysterics)*

STAR CAT: Let's get them out of that costume.

(They break away the siamese twin costume, freeing them. BETTINA *comforts* BERDINE. MRS. FORREST *enters)*

MRS. FORREST: I thought I'd find her here. I'm going to have all of you arrested for kidnapping.

STAR CAT: Mrs. Forrest, your daughter is mentally ill.

MRS. FORREST: My little girl is as normal as I am.

CHICKLET *(in the voice of* TYLENE): I gotta go back to work at the Safeway.

MRS. FORREST *(near hysteria, grasping at straws):* She wants to be an actress. She's putting on a character. *(Breaks down)* She's not sick!

CHICKLET *(as* ANN): You're so right, Mrs. Forrest, I am hardly the lunatic they are painting me to be. I am totally in control.

STAR CAT: You are merely a delusion of Chicklet Forrest that enables her to express anger and rage.

CHICKLET *(as* ANN): Fancy phrases. And a big basket. I'd like to strap you on sometime.

STAR CAT: That is highly unlikely since you are about to be obliterated.

CHICKLET *(as* ANN): Party pooper.

STAR CAT: You don't frighten me. I'm flesh and blood. You're a psychological manifestation. I can conquer you.

CHICKLET *(as* ANN): There's no man alive strong enough to conquer me . . . maybe Bob Hope.

STAR CAT: I'm going to place you under hypnosis and through the technique of past regression get to the root of the trauma that fragmented Chicklet's personality.

MRS. FORREST: I can't allow this. He doesn't know what he's doing.

PROVOLONEY: He's had three semesters of psychiatric training.

STAR CAT: Look into my eyes. I'm taking you back in time.

MRS. FORREST: Someone stop this madness!

CHICKLET (as ANN): Oh, shut your hole. Go on, darling Doctor Star Cat.

STAR CAT: I want to speak to Chicklet. Chicklet, are you there?

CHICKLET: It's hard, I feel so far away, I can't . . . (She begins to sound like a radio with static)

MRS. FORREST: She's babbling. (She exits)

STAR CAT: It's a bad connection. Chicklet, I know you are there. We are here to help you. Trust me. Are you there? (CHICKLET is sounding like a radio quickly switching stations)

KANAKA (sincerely): Maybe you should try her on FM.

STAR CAT: Talk to us Chicklet, talk to us.

CHICKLET (static noises clearing, as DR. ROSE): . . . lieve you will have greater success conversing with one of us.

cfs]star cat: Who am I talking to?

CHICKLET (as DR. ROSE): Dr. Rose Mayer, you're on the air.

STAR CAT: Who exactly are you?

CHICKLET (as DR. ROSE): A radio personality, and a syndicated columnist.

PROVOLONEY: This is weird, man, too weird.

CHICKLET (as DR. ROSE): I serve a very important function in Chicklet's life. Any situation that gets a little mishugga, that requires tact or diplomacy, I come in. In toto, I'm a people person.

STAR CAT: And who is Tylene?

CHICKLET (as TYLENE): I am her ambitious self. Come September first, I am attending night school where I can study keypunch and office management skills.

(Suddenly CHICKLET turns into STEVE, an all American boy)

CHICKLET (as STEVE): Whoa, can I just say something for a minute?

STAR CAT: I believe we're meeting someone new. What's your name?

CHICKLET (as STEVE): Steve.

STAR CAT: Are you also a radio personality?

CHICKLET (as STEVE): No. I'm a male model.

STAR CAT: Describe yourself.

CHICKLET (as STEVE): I'm a forty regular. (Fidgety) I'm very important to Chicklet. I'm her athletic self. I enjoy all sports, ice hockey, kayaking, golf, competition bowling. Of course I do try to be a well-rounded person. I love old romantic movies, snuggling up by a fire. I guess what I look most for in a girl are great legs and a sense of herself. (He winks at BETTINA, who gasps)

STAR CAT: Are there any more of you?

CHICKLET (as STEVE): Gosh, let's see, there's a veterinarian, a couple singers, a reformed rabbi, a lighting designer, the accounting firm of Edelman and Edelman, a podiatrist . . . (As CHICKLET) Help me.

STAR CAT: Chicklet, is that you?

CHICKLET *(as a little girl):* Uh huh. *(She sings)* "It's raining, it's pouring . . ."

STAR CAT: How old are you?

CHICKLET: Eight. Seven and a half.

STAR CAT: Where are you?

CHICKLET: In a room, Mama calls it the hotel. There's a playground across the street. My brother Frankie and me like to go on the swings.

BERDINE: She doesn't have a brother.

CHICKLET: I do too have a brother. He's seven and a half.

YO YO: Twins.

CHICKLET: Mama says we can't go on the swings alone. She says it's too dangerous. Mama's going to take us to the movies today. She says she's gonna . . .

(MRS. FORREST *appears in a strange light, she is in the past, dressed in a red dress like a sexy young whore in the 1940s*)

MRS. FORREST *(gently):* Baby, I'm so sorry. We're gonna have to go to the movies another day. Mama's gotta work. Fellas, come on in. These are my twins, ain't they cute?

CHICKLET: But you promised you'd take us to the movies.

MRS. FORREST: Well, I'm sorry. What do you want from my life? You wanna eat, don'tcha? Anyways, we gotta do our bit for the boys who go overseas. These guys are in the Navy and your Mama is making sure they are very well entertained. *(She giggles. To the children)* Now darlings, go outside and play. I'll meet you in the playground in an hour.

CHICKLET: You're not fair.

MRS. FORREST: Florence, I don't want anymore lip. Take Frankie and go outside and play. And don't you go near those swings. *(She turns to the sailors)* Sorry guys, being a Mom ain't easy. Now what was your name again, good looking? Pleased to meetcha, Johnny. Just call me Ann. Ann Bowman. *(She exits)*

CHICKLET *(in her normal voice):* I was so angry. I wanted to hurt her. I took Frankie's hand and we crossed the street to the playground. There were these awful slum children playing, pounding strange primitive instruments. A sharp breeze caused the wild flowers to have the wizened faces of starving circus clowns. The sky seemed so threatening, as if the clouds were created of demented angels warning me to flee. But I couldn't. I can't. Don't make me go on. Please.

STAR CAT: You must. What happened next?

CHICKLET: I look down and there's a pale green snake slithering along the crack of the pavement, a coolly seductive creature on its way to a lizard ball. This veridian temptress stops to deliver me a message. A perverse billet-doux that I must disobey my mother. No, no, I can't do that. I love my mother. She's kind and beautiful. The snakes multiply, in a moment, there are reptiles covering the jungle gym making those steel bars as green as grass and terrifyingly alive. And all of them whispering "Go on, go on, go on the swings. Your mother doesn't love you. She loathes the very sight of you." I looked at my little brother, wearing his red overalls with the little fishes. I said, "Frankie, let's go on the swings. It'll be fun. I don't care what Mama said." He got on the swing and I pushed him. Harder and harder I pushed him until he was soaring into the clouds and that's when I dared him. I dared him, "I bet you can't stay on with no hands." He took me up on the bet and let go, and my wonderful little twin brother, this adorable little boy who loved and trusted me, he flew off the swing and into the outstretched arms of those ghastly angels and I never saw him again until we found his crushed, little body in the dumpster next door!

(She dissolves into tears, STAR CAT *holds her.* MRS. FORREST *appears again as she is today)*

MRS. FORREST *(devastated):* It's all true. All of it true. I was so ashamed. I blamed myself for the death of my boy. But I always loved my little girl. *(To* CHICKLET) You must believe that. I did love you. I do. And when Chicklet lost her memory of that day, I took it as a blessing from God. I vowed to create a new life for us. I changed my name, moved to a new city. I suppose I tried too hard, went too far and now . . . now I see I'm doomed to failure.

CHICKLET: Mother, hold me. *(They embrace)*

BERDINE *(sobbing):* I was supposed to be her best friend, but I never knew.

KANAKA: How do you feel, Chicklet?

CHICKLET: As if a thousand doors have been opened.

PROVOLONEY: But what does this all mean?

STAR CAT: It's really very simple. Chicklet did her best to suppress this traumatic childhood episode by denying herself all normal human emotion, so she created various alter egos to express emotion for her. She associated the sex drive with her mother, so she in effect became her childhood vision of her mother, Ann Bowman, whenever placed in a potentially erotic situation.

KANAKA: Is this condition contagious?

STAR CAT: Indeed not. Over eighteen percent of all Americans suffer from some form of multiple personality disorder.

It is not communicable and in most cases, treatable with medical care.

BETTINA *(energetically):* This is the most exciting story I've ever heard. This is the project that's going to win me an Oscar.

PROVOLONEY: Huh?

BETTINA: A surfer girl with a split personality. A prestige picture if I ever saw one. *(To* CHICKLET*)* Honey, I want to option this property, and believe me I'll pay top dollar. I can't promise casting approval, but you can trust my integrity.

MRS. FORREST: I don't know. This is an invasion of . . .

CHICKLET: Mother, this is important. I want the public to know what it's like to suffer from a multiple personality disorder. And Berdine, will she be in the picture? She's very important, you know.

BETTINA: Oh, sure, sure, a character part.

STAR CAT: But Bettina, do you really think you're ready to interpret such a complex role?

BETTINA *(with artistic intensity):* I don't think, I feel. I know this girl. I feel her torment. I am Chicklet! *(Suddenly switching to her practical show business nature)* Yo Yo and Provoloney, I'm taking you to New York with me as technical consultants on the Malibu scene.

YO YO: Wow, New York!

PROVOLONEY: The Philharmonic!

YO YO: The New York City Ballet!

PROVOLONEY: Balanchine!

YO YO: The Frick! Provoloney, should we tell them about us?

PROVOLONEY: Yeah, since this is the time for truth telling. Yo Yo and I are lovers. *(Everyone gasps)*

YO YO: Yes, and we're proud of it. I've read all about the persecution of homosexuals, how in big cities, bars are raided and innocent people arrested, their lives ruined. But someday, someday we're going to fight back and the laws will be changed, and our brothers and sisters will march down the main streets of America shouting that we are proud to be who we are!

PROVOLONEY: Oh, Yo Yo, I really love you. *(They embrace. The crowd sighs in sympathy)*

BETTINA: Come on everybody, let's move this party to my place. I've got the best record collection in town. *(They all hoot and holler and exit except for* BERDINE)

BERDINE *(alone onstage, holding the siamese twin costume):* Life sure is wacky. Here Chicklet and I were best friends and I never really knew her. If I don't know *her,* can I ever truly know anyone? Star Cat thinks science can tell us everything and Bettina says if she feels things, they're true. Oh, sweet, lonely Schopenhauer and crazy ole Nietzsche and dear, committed Jean-Paul, all of you searching and never settling for an easy answer to life's eternal puzzlement. I hereby vow to carry on your never-ending quest. I know now that my true calling is to be a novelist and devote my life to exploring the fathomless possibilities of the human comedy. Hey, wait for Berdine! *(She runs off. Blackout.)*

Scene Ten

The beach at twilight. STAR CAT *is walking along the beach, wearing a tie and jacket.* KANAKA *enters carrying a suitcase.*

KANAKA: Hey, my man. It's time to shove off. You gonna say farewell to your old chum, Kanaka?

STAR CAT: You off to Tahiti?

KANAKA *(embarrassed):* No, uh not Tahiti, exactly.

STAR CAT: The Ivory Coast?

KANAKA: New York.

STAR CAT: New York. What kind of place is that for the King of the Surfers?

KANAKA: Bettina. She wants me with her. She needs me.

STAR CAT: I had no idea. You and Bettina.

KANAKA: Yeah well, you know Bettina and her incredible instincts about people. She says our personalities sort of fit together like a crazy jigsaw puzzle. But I told her, I'm the kind of guy that needs my freedom. I don't put up with no bunk, no star tantrums.

(From offstage, we hear BETTINA *shouting like a fishwife)*

BETTINA: Kanaka! Don't keep me waiting! We've got a nine o'clock plane to catch and I'm not missing it on account of some slow as molasses beach bum. Move it!

KANAKA *(subserviant):* Yes, Bettina. *(To* STAR CAT) Ciaou, kid. *(He exits)*

STAR CAT *(to himself):* The great Kanaka. What a mystery.

*(*CHICKLET *appears in a beautiful gown, somehow grown up and lovely)*

CHICKLET: Good evening, Star Cat.

STAR CAT *(in shock):* Chicklet?

CHICKLET: It's a beautiful night. The King of the Sea must be having cocktails.

STAR CAT: Chicklet, you've become a young woman.

CHICKLET: Have I? Star Cat, I . . .

STAR CAT: I'm not Star Cat anymore. Call me Herbert. Herbert Mullin. Everything seems so different now. I'm leaving the beach.

CHICKLET: Where are you going?

STAR CAT: Back to college. I think I could make a good psychiatrist.

CHICKLET: Do you really want to, with all your heart?

STAR CAT: I do. I want to make sure a monster like Ann Bowman never appears again.

CHICKLET: I'll miss you, Star Cat . . . I mean, Herb.

STAR CAT: I was wondering . . . would you wear my pin?

CHICKLET *(thrilled):* Your pin. Does this mean we're exclusive?

STAR CAT: Well, I'll be all the way in Boston. You can't expect a guy to . . .

CHICKLET *(mad):* Well, forget it, you creep. I'll be darned if I'll keep the home fires burning while you're pawing some Beacon Hill blueblooded beasel.

STAR CAT: That sounds like Ann Bowman.

CHICKLET: I hope so.

STAR CAT: You're quite a girl. The only girl for me. So will you wear my pin?

CHICKLET: Will I ever! It's the ultimate. It positively surpasses every living emotion I've ever had! *(She whirls around and takes his arm and they walk down the surf to their new happiness. Blackout.)*

THE END

Scene One
Alternate Beginning

The beach. YO YO *and* NICKY *are playing with a beach ball, but staring at a girl out front.*

YO YO: Nicky, look at that chick in the white bikini. She really knows how to shake those maracas.

NICKY: Look at that butt.

YO YO: Summer gives me a one–track mind.

(PROVOLONEY *enters)*

PROVOLONEY: Girls! Girls! Girls!

YO YO: Hey there, Provoloney!

PROVOLONEY: What a fantabulous day.

NICKY: Aw shoot, I gotta go get back to work at that malt shop. My lunch break is almost over.

YO YO: Call in sick.

PROVOLONEY: Say you were run over by a hit-and-run surfer.

NICKY: Nah, old Augie's a great guy. I couldn't let him down.

(STAR CAT *enters*)

YO YO: Hey, Star Cat, how's my man?

STAR CAT: What are you clowns doing? Those waves are as high as Mount Everest.

PROVOLONEY *(looks out):* Oh wow, look at them, man.

STAR CAT: It's time to hit the water.

NICKY: It's more BLTs for me. See ya, fellas. Gosh, I'm so happy! *(Exits.)*

STAR CAT: Come on guys, grab your boards, it's time to shoot the curl.

PROVOLONEY: Hot diggity! *(They all run offstage)*

SLEEPING BEAUTY OR COMA*

Vampire LESBIANS of SODOM

SLEEPING BEAUTY *or Coma* and VAMPIRE LESBIANS OF SODOM were presented at the Provincetown Playhouse in New York City on June 19, 1985. They were directed by Kenneth Elliott. Scenic design was by B.T. Whitehill, costume design by John Glaser, lighting design by Vivien Leone. Hair design was by Elizabeth Katherine Carr who also acted as Production Stage Manager. Choreography was by Jeff Veazey. The cast of SLEEPING BEAUTY *or Coma* was as follows:

Miss Thick . . . . Andy Halliday
Enid Wetwhistle . . . . Meghan Robinson
Sebastian Lore . . . . Kenneth Elliott
Fauna Alexander . . . . Charles Busch
Ian McKenzie . . . . Tom Aulino
Anthea Arlo . . . . Theresa Marlowe
Barry Posner . . . . Robert Carey
Craig Prince . . . . Arnie Kolodner

The action takes place in and around London in the 1960s.

The cast of VAMPIRE LESBIANS OF SODOM was as follows:

Ali, a guard . . . . Robert Carey
Hujar, a guard . . . . Arnie Kolodner
A virgin sacrifice . . . . Charles Busch
The Succubus, a monster . . . . Meghan Robinson
King Carlisle, a silent movie idol . . . . . . Kenneth Elliott
Etienne, a butler . . . . Andy Halliday
Renee Vain, a starlet . . . . Theresa Marlowe
La Condesa, a silent screen vamp . . . . . . Meghan Robinson

Madeleine Astarté, a stage actress . . . . . . Charles Busch
Oatsie Carewe, a gossip columnist . . . . . Tom Aulino
Zack, a chorus boy . . . . Arnie Kolodner
P.J., a chorus boy . . . . Robert Carey
Danny, a chorus boy . . . . Andy Halliday
Tracy, an aspiring singer . . . . Theresa Marlowe

Synopsis of Scenes

Scene 1: Sodom, in days of old. The entrance to a forbidding cave.

Scene 2: Hollywood, 1920. La Condesa's mansion.

Scene 3: Las Vegas today. A rehearsal hall.

AUTHOR'S NOTE

There are elements of fairy tales in these two one-act plays and there is a fairy tale quality to the story behind their creation. I wrote them to be performed by me and a close group of friends for one weekend in a bar called The Limbo Lounge on the lower east side of Manhattan. The performance was planned more as a party than as a professional event. The entire budget for the show was thirty six dollars. There was no stage and the lighting was composed of two sun lamps. The costumes were created from the more outlandish items in my Aunt Lillian's closet.

The act of putting on a play for the simple joy of it created a magical excitement in the room that night. We scheduled more performances and our little troupe became known as Theatre-In-Limbo. We soon developed a faithful cult audience, and it became clear that our "party" had commercial possibilities. We produced the show Off-Broadway. Like all good fairy tales, ours had a happy ending: a very long and prosperous run.

Along with the innocence of fairy tale, these plays also have qualities of old fashioned burlesque sketches. They are full of opportunities for double takes, sculls, pratfalls and other comic "schtick." They should be played flamboyantly, with a sense of almost operatic intensity, but more important with honesty and a sense of reality. Nothing will kill the humor of these pieces more quickly than performers who "wink at the audience" and signal that they are in on the joke.

In the original production, several of the female roles were played by men in drag. This is not necessary and I believe any rearrangement of gender could be successful. If men are to play some of the female roles, I think it is important that they seek out the real human qualities of these characters and not overdo their grotesqueness or bitchiness. These women are old–fashioned heroines, and it's my aim that in both plays the audience should be touched by the characters' renewed bond of friendship. It is that same bond of friendship that I found in Theatre-In-Limbo and which inspired this work.

PRODUCTION NOTES

Both VAMPIRE LESBIANS OF SODOM and SLEEPING BEAUTY *or Coma* were played on a bare stage. They were presented on a proscenium stage with footlights to give the feel of an old vaudeville show. I do feel that the plays could be successfully performed in a variety of stage configurations.

The backdrop for SLEEPING BEAUTY *or Coma* was a blow–up of a page from a fashion designers' sketch pad, complete with a large swatch of fabric pinned to the drop with a giant safety pin. The sketch was of a very "mod" female fashion figure. There was also a large face of a girl with big eyes surrounded by Twiggy lashes. At key moments in the play, the eyes would close and open.

In VAMPIRE LESBIANS OF SODOM, we used one backdrop that changed during each scene. In Sodom, there was a silhouette of a mountainous terrain. In Hollywood, a cut out of the Hollywood sign was placed over the mountains and in Las Vegas, a flashy sign of various gambling symbols covered up the Hollywood sign.

The lack of furniture and set pieces suited our shoestring budget, but also allowed us to go from scene to scene with speed and fluidity.

SUGGESTED DOUBLING OF ROLES

Actor One . . . . Miss Thick, Etienne, Danny
Actor Two . . . . Enid, La Condesa
Actor Three . . . . Sebastian, King
Actor Four . . . . Fauna, Madeleine
Actor Five . . . . Ian, Oatsie
Actor Six . . . . Barry, Ali, P.J.
Actor Seven . . . . Anthea, Renee
Actor Eight .Craig, Hujar, Zach

Enid Wetwhistle (Carole Monferdini, at right) is thrilled to meet two rising stars in the fashion firmament, designer Fauna Alexander (David Drake, center) and photographer Ian McKenzie (Matt Bradford Sullivan).

Photo by T.L. Boston

SLEEPING BEAUTY OR COMA

Scene One

*1966, London. The fashion house of Sebastian Loré [LORAY].
The entire play takes place before a backdrop of a giant fashion sketch. It's a drawing of a full length fashion figure and
also a close up of a girl's face with big eyes surrounded by
Twiggy type lashes.* MISS THICK, SEBASTIAN's *spinsterish secretary enters followed by* ENID, *a pretty young typist.*

MISS THICK: It won't do. It simply won't do.

ENID: All the girls at the temp agency wear mini-skirts. It's the
rage.

MISS THICK: Disgusting.

ENID: This is 1966, you know. It's a new age. You should get
yourself a micro-mini. You've got smashing pins.

MISS THICK: If a young man ogled my loins, I'd have his eyes
gouged out with a fiery poker. You've come on a very bad

day. We've lost our top model and we must find a new girl by this afternoon. Mr. Loré has yet to hear the news.

ENID: Sebastian Loré. He's the top fashion designer in the world. Me lallies are turning to water.

MISS THICK: Oh, pook. There's nothing to be nervous about. *(A bloodcurdling scream is heard offstage)* He's just heard about Lucinda Blake. Five, four, three, two, one, blast off!

(SEBASTIAN LORÉ *enters. He is an older man of great stature and manic energy. He is dressed flamboyantly, but in a manner redolent of a past era)*

SEBASTIAN: How dare Lucinda Blake refuse to model my fall collection. She can't do this to me! It's a plot, I tell you. Mini–skirts, those ghastly mop–headed singers, Carnaby Street. It's a plot to destroy me. Mark my words, Lucinda Blake shall regret this day.

MISS THICK: Oh Mr. Loré, not another law suit.

SEBASTIAN: No, disembowelment. I smell a foreign presence. *(Sees* ENID) What is this?

MISS THICK: The girl from the office temp service.

SEBASTIAN: Cover your thighs at once, girl.

ENID: I think mini-skirts are super.

SEBASTIAN: A woman's body must be covered from head to toe. Shackle the breasts, cinch in the waist, bind the legs. That is my fashion statement.

ENID: Aren't you going to ask my name?

SEBASTIAN: Not likely.

ENID: Enid Wetwhistle.

MISS THICK: Miss Wetwhistle, if you would . . .

ENID: Enid, Miss Thick, Enid. I was named after me mum's leg waxer.

SEBASTIAN: Such stories, your name ought to be Scheherezade. Thick, here are photos of the girls we saw last week. Perhaps one of them will do.

ENID: I don't think so. This one looks dead grotty. Grotty, grotesque. You can't have a tuned–out dolly with a size–ten hooter parading in such top gear rags. Ooooh, she looks like a real mixer.

SEBASTIAN *(coolly to* THICK): The child's daft.

MISS THICK: No Mr. L., it's the new lingo, mod talk. It comes from the youth gangs, the mods and the rockers.

SEBASTIAN: My dear, do you think you could master an imitation of a deaf mute, with the emphasis on the latter?

ENID: That's very funny. Would you like me to take a letter?

SEBASTIAN: I would like you to take a personality suppressant.

MISS THICK: Mrs. Arlo should be here any minute.

SEBASTIAN: Oh yes, the very modern Anthea Arlo. She needs a gown for her anniversary. I trust that impossible sketch artist has been hard at work.

MISS THICK: Yes, Miss Alexander is indeed in the back feverishly sketching. She is quite an eccentric young lady.

SEBASTIAN: How so?

MISS THICK: Last week she told me she would like to get to know me better. She then proceeded to examine my scalp for bumps.

SEBASTIAN: Bumps?

MISS THICK: She then informed me that in a previous lifetime, I had been a cossack with a peg leg and an hyperactive penis.

SEBASTIAN: Have you seen the sketches for Mrs. Arlo?

MISS THICK: No and I don't believe they exist.

SEBASTIAN: I would like to have a word with this fanciful young lady. Bring her in.

MISS THICK: Miss Alexander, Mr. Loré would like to see you immediately. (THICK *exits*)

ENID: I think I'm going to like working here. You're a very colorful character. I write stories in my spare time. Stories and poems.

SEBASTIAN: Do you?

ENID: Yes, perhaps someday I'll write a story about you and make a mint.

SEBASTIAN: Try it! That's all, just try it! Miss Alexander, would you come in here immediately! (FAUNA *and* MISS THICK *enter.* FAUNA *is a struggling young designer dressed in an outrageous smock of her own design. She is the embodiment of the new mod look)* Mrs. Arlo is arriving momentarily and I understand we have no sketches to show her. Who is to blame? Surely not I. Not Miss Thick. You! You! You are to blame for this disaster and yet I suppose you want sympathy.

FAUNA: Oh yes, scads of sympathy. This has been the worst week of my entire life. *(Sees* ENID*)* Oh my God, Clotilde!

ENID: No, I'm Enid. Enid Wetwhistle.

FAUNA: My dear, you and I were best friends a long, long time ago.

ENID: Really, when?

FAUNA: 1792. We were seamstresses in Paris during the revolution. We were involved in this royalist conspiracy and well, I hate to be the one to tell you this, we were both guillotined the same day. Hardly a groovy scene. Do you ever get neck pains?

ENID: Well, when it rains . . .

SEBASTIAN: I have a terrible pain in my neck.

FAUNA: Oh Mr. Loré, you and I go back even further.

SEBASTIAN: Miss Alexander, I have not time to—

FAUNA: Ancient Mesopotamia. You were my sister-in-law.

SEBASTIAN: I am flattered that you—

FAUNA: We buried you alive. You were an evil woman.

SEBASTIAN (exploding): Enough! I have had enough of your addlepated lunacy. Where are those sketches?

FAUNA (intimidated): Now Mr. Loré, I promise you when Mrs. Arlo arrives, you will have your sketches.

SEBASTIAN: And they better damn well be brilliant.

FAUNA: Yes sir.

(The door buzzes)

SEBASTIAN: That must be Mrs. Arlo. Thick detain her while this nitwit gets those sketches together.

MISS THICK: Yes Mr. L. *(She exits)*

SEBASTIAN *(to* ENID*)*: You, come with me. I'm about to bury you alive in a file cabinet. (SEBASTIAN *and* ENID *exit*)

FAUNA: Psst!

(IAN MCKENZIE *pops in.* IAN *is a very "now" young photographer*)

IAN: Thank God, they've left. It was getting damned icy on that bloody fire escape.

FAUNA: Where are the sketches?

IAN: Here you go, luv.

FAUNA: Did you find the sketch of the dress with the popcorn balls?

IAN: It's in with the others. I hope you pull this off, luv.

FAUNA: Now all I have to do is slip my designs into the stack of Sebastian Loré sketches and pray that Anthea Arlo chooses mine.

(Offstage laughter is heard)

IAN: I think I hear them coming. I'll get back on the fire escape.

FAUNA: I'll get the rest of the sketches.

(They exit as SEBASTIAN, MISS THICK *and the glamorous* ANTHEA ARLO *enter.* ANTHEA ARLO *is a London socialite dressed in the elegantly conservative Sebastian Loré manner)*

ANTHEA: Now Sebastian darling, I don't have all day. Don't keep me in suspense, I want to see the sketches. This dress must be super spectacular. A girl celebrates her fourth second wedding anniversary only once in a lifetime.

SEBASTIAN *(with unctuous charm):* I believe you will be quite pleased with these sketches. All arrogance aside, I am quite at the peak of my genius. Miss Thick, would you please tell Miss Alexander we're ready for the sketches. (MISS THICK *exits.)*

ANTHEA: Now you did promise me something new and extravagant. There's something vital and catching in the London air, don't you feel it?

SEBASTIAN: It's called streptococci.

(MISS THICK *and* FAUNA *enter with the sketches)*

MISS THICK: Here they are, sir.

ANTHEA: May I? *(She takes the sketches and looks through them)*

SEBASTIAN: The lime green crepe will look divine with the Arlo diamonds.

ANTHEA: It doesn't say anything to me. What about this one. *(She look at the next sketch)*

SEBASTIAN: This one is quite a novelty. Notice the severity of the bateau neck.

ANTHEA: But Sebastian, you've been showing me bateau necks for five seasons now.

SEBASTIAN *(haughtily):* A bateau neckline is one of my signatures.

ANTHEA: I suppose I'm being unfair. I want you to be something you're not. My friends have been urging me to find another designer, but we've had such a successful working relationship in the past.

SEBASTIAN: My dear Mrs. Arlo, do you want to go down in history as a woman of great style or do you want to be known as a flibbertygibbet who grasps onto the latest rage?

ANTHEA: I don't want to go down in history as an old fart. I'm sorry Sebastian, but these will not do. Look at this gown, you've been doing variations of that same satin sheath for years. And look at . . . *(She flips to the next sketch and is in shock)* Oh my . . . Oh my . . .

MISS THICK: Is something the matter?

ANTHEA: This number is spectacular. Look how short the hemline is. *(Confused)* Do I dare? *(Thrilled)* It's darling!

SEBASTIAN: Why, this isn't my . . .

ANTHEA: What's it made of?

FAUNA: Mr. Loré, that's the one you told me to do in crushed velvet.

SEBASTIAN: I?

ANTHEA: I adore it. An antique fabric in a modern style. Sebastian, you are a genius. And a terribly sly fox. Oh, look at this one. A bare midriff? Where could I wear it? I'll wear it everywhere. *(Looks at another sketch)* This is fabulous. Sebastian, what are these round balls attached to it?

FAUNA: Mr. Loré, I believe they're made of popcorn?

ANTHEA: Popcorn balls on an evening gown. I'll wear it to the opening of the Hungarian Film Festival. Sebastian, my husband will kill me, but please make them all up for me. Of course, none of the frumpy old fashioned stuff, but that was meant as a joke, wasn't it?

SEBASTIAN *(seething):* A feeble joke.

ANTHEA: I must say, a visit to your atelier is full of surprises.

SEBASTIAN: Surprises for all of us. I'll have my staff get started on all of these. Miss Thick will be calling you in two weeks for fittings.

ANTHEA: I can hardly wait. This will be so much fun. I'll leave you to your work. Sebastian, I can hardly tell you how thrilled I am for you. A whole new career shall be yours and even greater than your past.

SEBASTIAN: Miss Thick will show you out. Good day, Mrs. Arlo.

ANTHEA: Goodbye and thank you again. (MISS THICK *and* ANTHEA *exit)*

SEBASTIAN: Well, well, well, aren't we full of mischief?

FAUNA *(frightened):* She liked the sketches.

SEBASTIAN: My new career shall be even greater than my past.

FAUNA: Does that mean you're going to let me design for your label?

SEBASTIAN: It means that I shall make those dresses for that foolish woman and then you're fired! You tried to make a fool out of me. Well, nobody makes a fool of Sebastian Loré.

FAUNA: I was just trying to get a break.

SEBASTIAN: I shall be a great help to your budding career. I shall see to it that no other fashion house will ever hire you. I suggest, my dear, you apply your ambition to another line of work.

FAUNA (*reaching for the sketches*): Then I shall take my designs with me.

SEBASTIAN: Those are my designs. I believe you've forgotten the document you signed the day I took you on. All designs created under my employ are the undisputed original work of Sebastian Loré.

FAUNA: You wouldn't.

SEBASTIAN: I have. So any foolish idea of yours to contact Anthea Arlo will result in nothing more than a painful lawsuit.

FAUNA: You won't get away with this.

(IAN *enters*)

IAN: Fauna, are you all right?

SEBASTIAN: And who is this young hoodlum evidently hiding on my fire escape?

FAUNA: Ian McKenzie, my flat mate.

IAN: I overheard this entire scene and I'll make sure the papers learn how the legendary Sebastian Loré tried to destroy a young designer. You old people are all the same. You can't even see that your time is over. Fauna makes clothes that kids need to wear today, and doesn't turn them into high fashion zombies like you do.

SEBASTIAN: Miss Thick. (MISS THICK *enters*) Please ring the police and inform them a burglar has climbed in through our fire escape. (THICK *exits*)

FAUNA: We're going. Come, Ian. Mr. Loré, it's been perfectly enchanting working for you and I hope your fabled bateau neckline tightens and chokes you! (FAUNA *and* IAN *exit*)

SEBASTIAN: Back to work. Thick, give me those composites. (THICK *enters with photos*) We must find a new girl by this afternoon.

ENID *(enters with a large bolt of fabric):* Excuse me, I found this bolt of fabric stuck away in a corner. It would make super curtains for me flat. I was wondering if you were just trashing it.

MISS THICK *(snatching the fabric away):* Foolish girl, that is new fabric for the spring evening wear.

SEBASTIAN: Are you telling me that that disgusting, tawdry, loathsome fabric was ordered for my evening wear?

MISS THICK: It matches the swatches.

SEBASTIAN: No, it doesn't, you evil whore. That is not the fabric I ordered.

MISS THICK *(throwing it to the ground):* I can take no more of this hysteria. I am handing in my resignation.

ENID: Oh, Miss Thick.

SEBASTIAN: You will not quit. I shall bring you to court.

MISS THICK: Bring me to court and I shall plead insanity!

SEBASTIAN: You are not mad. I am going mad! The hell with litigation, I shall murder you first!

MISS THICK: Murder away! (SEBASTIAN *chokes her*)

ENID: Excuse me, are you trashing it then?

SEBASTIAN: Yes, yes, take the bloody lot of it! *(Calmed down, looking at photos)* Jane Fitzhugh. Is she available for the shoot?

MISS THICK: Her libel suit against you goes to court next week.

SEBASTIAN: Gail Markham.

MISS THICK: Drying out.

(ENID *drapes the fabric around herself as a way of measuring it for drapes)*

SEBASTIAN: Lisa Gardiner.

MISS THICK: Living in Pittsburgh.

SEBASTIAN: Maxine Dellafroie?

MISS THICK: Don't you remember? She's the one with the castration fantasies about you.

SEBASTIAN: No, I don't think she'll do. Tamara.

MISS THICK: Tried to poison you at last year's Christmas party.

SEBASTIAN: That one has a temper. *(He notices* ENID *swathed in the fabric)* Thick! Look!

MISS THICK: Where?

SEBASTIAN: There. Look what she's doing.

MISS THICK: I see nothing but an office temporary.

SEBASTIAN: She's it. She's our girl. She shall represent my fashion line around the world. Her face flashed upon a thousand magazines. Child, what was your name again?

ENID *(in shock):* Enid Wetwhistle.

SEBASTIAN: It needs a name, a name Thick, give me a name.

MISS THICK: Let me fetch a doctor.

SEBASTIAN: She is the flower of fashion, ready to bloom. A delicate bud among thorns, waiting to be picked. A rose. A rose. That's it. From now on, my girl, you are Rose!

(Blackout.)

Scene Two

SEBASTIAN LORÉ's *fashion show.* SEBASTIAN *is addressing the audience.*

SEBASTIAN: Ladies and gentlemen of the press, please do not stand. These past few months have been filled with fetes and festivities celebrating my twentieth anniversary as the czar of fashion. Still, I feel my greatest work is ahead of me. As I gave the women of the world a new look in 1946, today in 1966, I shall present womankind with a brand new image. And with a new image, there must be a new woman. I have found her in a young girl I call Rose. And tonight I give her to you. (MISS THICK *tiptoes out onstage, unbeknownst to* SEBASTIAN. *She tries to get his attention. The spotlight hits her, she freezes)* The first number Rose will be modeling is a new adaptation of my classic satin sheath, cut on the bias, with the Loré bateau neck and a trim of gold beadwork. Note the detail of . . . (SEBASTIAN *turns and sees* THICK *and screams)* Thick! How dare you show your face in public.

MISS THICK: Mr. L, we have a problem.

SEBASTIAN *(whispering):* What is it? Where's Rose? (MISS THICK *whispers to him)* What? *(She whispers again)* I can't understand you.

MISS THICK *(screaming in frustration):* She's fucking bolted!

SEBASTIAN: She's gone? *(He begins to twitch and laugh uncontrollably)*

MISS THICK: Mr. L, get a hold of yourself.

SEBASTIAN: Very amusing. Oh yes, this is all very amusing. A great, big joke has been played upon Sebastian Loré. *(Muttering to himself in the voice of his mother)* Sebastian, you don't want to play with dolls. *(As himself as a child)* Mama? Mama? *(As his cockney mother)* I won't have you ripping apart my dresses. *(Himself as a child)* Mama? Mama? *(As his mother)* What sort of boy is this?

MISS THICK *(trying to get him offstage):* Come this way, Mr. L.

SEBASTIAN *(in mad fury):* Get your hands off me! No one does this to Sebastian Loré. No one makes a fool of me and lives. Enid Wetwhistle, you will be sorry for this!

(Blackout.)

Scene Three

A wild chase ensues to the music of 1960s British rock and roll. It should have the feel of a frenetic Richard Lester film of the period. ENID *runs across the stage in a plastic rain slicker. When she exits,* SEBASTIAN *and* MISS THICK *enter, one looking left, the other looking right.* SEBASTIAN *pantomimes for her search stage right, while he goes stage left. They exit. From stage left, three youths wearing Pierrot masks run on carrying signs saying, "Down With No!" and "Now is Here!" They chant their slogans as they exit stage left.* SEBASTIAN *and* MISS THICK *enter stage left, their faces covered by open copies of the London Times.* ENID *enters stage right, wearing Groucho glasses with a fake nose and moustache. Not recognizing her pursuers, she taps* MISS THICK *on the shoulder. The two villains lower their newspapers. They too are wearing Groucho glasses.* ENID *makes a run for it stage right, with* THICK *and* SEBASTIAN *in hot pursuit. The youthful protesters enter stage left and cross the stage again. A strobe light begins to flicker making the stage look like a silent movie.* ENID *runs on from stage right followed by* MISS THICK *holding a butterfly net and* SEBAS-TIAN. *They circle the stage and exit right.* ENID *immediately enters again followed by the evil duo with this time* SEBASTIAN *holding the net. The protesters join them from stage right and confusion reigns. In the mayhem,* ENID *escapes. The protesters follow her offstage, leaving behind a foiled* SEBASTIAN *with only* MISS THICK *trapped in the butterfly net. Blackout.)*

Scene Four

FAUNA *is being interviewed for a television documentary.*

FAUNA: Darlings, I'm absolutely thrilled that the BBC wants to
do a documentary on me, but where do I start? What year?
(Thoughtfully) What century? Well, you know, I once
worked for Sebastian Loré, till he fired me. Oh, those days
were grim, living off tinned ravioli, wearing my heels to flats
looking for a job. Till miraculously I inherited the lease to a
storefront and lo and behold, Fauna's Boutique was born. Ian
was having a terrible time making a go of it as a fashion
photographer. It was so unfair because his ideas were exciting and unlike anything that had been seen before.

(In a flashback, FAUNA *and* IAN *are seen on a rainy London
street.* IAN *is holding an umbrella)*

IAN: Oh Fauna, perhaps me Dad is right. Perhaps I'm not cut
out to be a fashion photographer.

FAUNA: Darling, you're a marvelous photographer. Don't be so negative. *(Embarrassed at her bad pun)* At least it stopped raining.

IAN *(putting down the umbrella):* It's such a vicious circle. I can't get the big fashion shoots because I don't have the experience and I can't get the experience because I can't find the work.

FAUNA: If it's any comfort to you, I think you've been doing some brilliant portraiture.

IAN: I'm shooting mug shots for the penitentiary.

(ENID *runs on crying, looking around furtively)*

IAN: That bird looks in trouble.

FAUNA: Ian, I know her. *(Calls out)* Excuse me darling, but don't I know you from somewhere?

ENID: Oh yes. Paris, a long time ago.

FAUNA: Yes, of course, Clotilde. But I've seen you since then, haven't I?

ENID: Sebastian Loré's studio.

FAUNA: Oh yes. But where are you off to now? You look as if you were being chased by the Gestapo.

IAN: Don't be nosey, Fauna.

ENID: You're not far from the truth. After you left, Sebastian discovered me.

FAUNA *(suspiciously):* Doing what?

ENID: No, you don't understand. He discovered me. I'm to be his top model.

IAN: You must be Rose.

FAUNA: The new mystery girl. We've read all about you in the paper. But isn't tonight your big debut?

ENID: Yes. *(She breaks down sobbing)*

IAN: Luv, you've just got stage fright, that's all.

FAUNA: It's more than that. I can tell.

ENID: He's trying to turn me into something I'm not. He hates me, Enid Wetwhistle. It's this strange Rose character that he's obsessed with. And he wants me to live her twenty-four hours a day. I can't do it.

FAUNA: Oh, the monster.

IAN: I think I read it starts at eight. You're late already.

ENID: I can't go. Once he presents me to the press there will be no escape.

FAUNA: Don't go!

IAN: Fauna, don't get any strange ideas in your head.

FAUNA: I'm not getting them in my head. I'm feeling vibrations throughout my body. You're coming home with us. The three of us were meant to meet out here tonight. Something important and wonderful is going to happen to all of us. Where do you live?

ENID: Well, nowhere. I can't go home. He'll find me there.

FAUNA: It's too perfect. We share a flat above a Chinese restaurant. I hope you don't mind the smell of chop suey.

IAN: It's the smell of chop suey mixed with Yardley's Eau de London that's fairly nauseating.

ENID: You'd really take me in?

FAUNA: Darling, face it, you're in! *(The three turn around, their backs to the audience and are caught in a freize in silhouette. Blackout.)*

Scene Five

This is what is called "the happiness sequence." To the speeded up recording of Wagner's "Overture to Act III of Lohengrin," the lights come up on FAUNA *skipping about joyfully holding a bouquet of flowers.* IAN *is holding up* ENID's *legs as they do a "wheelbarrow" walk across the stage. Blackout. Lights come up on the trio in a pyramid formation.* IAN *is stradling* ENID *and* FAUNA's *backs.* FAUNA *on her knees looks disconcerted. Blackout. Lights come up and* IAN *and* FAUNA *are miming a tennis match with* ENID *the enthusiastic fan. Blackout. Lights come up and the three are dancing in a frenzied conga line. Blackout. The light comes up and the three are frozen in a wacky pose. Each balanced on one leg with their other leg extended out and arms fanning out. Each one stands behind the other. They quickly lose their balance and fall to the ground laughing at their own foolishness. (Blackout.)*

Scene Six

FAUNA *and* IAN's *flat.* FAUNA *is seated on the floor painting her nails.* ENID *is pacing.*

ENID: Fauna, I have no direction in my life. I don't think I even have a personality.

FAUNA: Of course you have a personality.

ENID *(sits on the floor):* I don't know who I am. I'm a chameleon. I take on the colors of whoever I'm with. When I'm with you I even begin to think I'm psychic when I'm really just your sidekick.

FAUNA: You're right. You lack direction. When I look at you I see the number five thousand in an eastern direction.

ENID *(blankly):* I don't know what you're talking about.

FAUNA: Now I may be off a digit, but I think you should take a trip. Now it could be five thousand feet from here which I believe would land you in Trafalgar Square. But then it could be five thousand miles from here which . . . I wonder if there's much call for temp typists in Bora Bora?

ENID *(laughs and embraces* FAUNA): Oh Fauna, I adore you. Fauna, why did you pull away?

FAUNA: Did I?

ENID: Yes, what's wrong?

FAUNA *(extremely vulnerable):* I suddenly have this urge to kiss you. I've never felt this way about another woman.

ENID: Then kiss me. *(They tentatively move closer and gently kiss)*

FAUNA: Oh dear, does that make me a lesbian? (ENID *holds her)*

ENID *(tenderly and softly):* Oh Fauna, you're not a lesbian. You're just lonely and want to be loved.

FAUNA: Yes. More than anything I want to have a baby.

ENID: Then you shall have a baby.

FAUNA: I don't know. I've had several abortions.

ENID: How many?

FAUNA *(deadpan):* Forty-two.

ENID: Good things will happen to you. I just know it.

(IAN *enters wearing his camera around his neck)*

IAN: I haven't worked in weeks. I simply must take some photos. Fauna, how about posing?

FAUNA: Darling, I'm beat.

ENID: I'll pose for you.

IAN: You would?

FAUNA: He'll want you to do nudies, he always does. It's for his art, you know.

ENID: I'll pose nude for you.

IAN: I'd never dream of asking you.

ENID: That's why I will.

FAUNA: This is my cue to pop off to Dreamland. Ta, darlings. *(She exits)*

ENID: *(calling to her):* See you in the morning. *(To* IAN*)* How do you want me, Ian?

IAN: Just the way you are. *(He begins clicking photos.* ENID *begins assuming fashion poses.* IAN *follows her every move)* That's good. Great. You're a born model. Go, go, go. *(She shakes her hair seductively)* Great! Move, move. *(She strikes more poses)* Fabulous, move, move. *(She gets on her knees)* Stroke yourself. *(She follows his directions)* The hair, the face. Hand up just a bit. That's it, fabulous. *(He kisses her on the neck, then gets up)* Come at me now. Rethink it, rethink it. *(*ENID *pauses for a brief moment and then removes her blouse, her back visible to the audience. She crosses her arms over her breasts)* Fabulous. Hold it. On your back. *(She lies down, writhing on the floor)* Keep moving. Keep working. *(*IAN *kneels over her body coming in closer)* Head up towards me just a bit. *(*IAN *kisses her again on the neck, she caresses his thighs)* Fabulous, more eyes, more eyes. *(*IAN *and* ENID *are keyed up to a pitch of excitement similar in feeling to a sex act)* That's it! That's it! Oh my God, that's it! *(They freeze the pose of* IAN *straddling her in ecstasy. Blackout. The* *lights come up on* FAUNA *stage left, back in her interview with the BBC)*

FAUNA: That was the photo that changed our lives. Ian sold it as a record album cover for the rock band, Dandelion. The record and the photo created a sensation and sold five million copies. Everyone wanted to know who the mystery girl was.

Scene Seven

In flashback, FAUNA's *and* IAN's *flat.*

FAUNA: She simply has to come forth.

IAN: But what about Sebastian Loré? He must be livid with her.

FAUNA: Soon she'll be as famous as he is. As it is, she can't walk down the street without creating a mob scene. She's going to need a new name. Enid Wetwhistle does not wash with her image.

IAN *(wearily):* How about Rose?

FAUNA: Ian, I hope you're not implying that I'm exploiting her like that ghastly Sebastian Loré.

IAN: Don't be so sensitive.

FAUNA: Actually, Rose isn't such a bad name at that. But it's a bit too pallid, too cozy. She needs something with more bite. I've got it, Briar Rose.

FAUNA *(at her interview):* Briar Rose became the new modeling sensation. She was signed by a top agency and soon became the highest paid international model. I was still unknown. However, when I organized my first fashion show, Rose insisted on being my runway model. Because of her, my opening became a monster media event and my career as a designer skyrocketed. So did Ian's. His photographs of Briar Rose modeling Fauna Alexander's creation became the emblem of swinging mod London.

(FAUNA *exits as* ENID *makes a big entrance modeling at a fashion show. She's wearing a fabulous cape which she opens and then drops to the floor. Under it, she is wearing a long tight dress. With great panache, she removes the long skirt from the dress and is now in a micro mini skirt. She picks up the long skirt, swings it over her shoulder and exits triumphantly)*

Scene Eight

1969, three years later, IAN *is drinking at a pub.*

IAN: Who are you? Just what I thought. Another bloody jour-
nalist. Look man, everything's been said already. The lousy
scandal sheets have been full of it. Sorry, mate. Sorry for
jumping at you like that. I'm sure your job's none too easy. Of
course, the headlines, "Wild Nights at the Top," "The True
Story at Last" mean nothing. Can it be only three years since
we all became rich and famous? You reporters don't know
the half of it. You weren't there that night. I was. I was there
and I couldn't do anything to prevent it. Anthea Arlo threw a
lavish birthday party for Briar Rose at the Ad Lib Club. A
night I wish I could forget.

(FLASHBACK *to the party.* ANTHEA *enters garbed in the wildest
excesses of 60s chic*)

ANTHEA: Ian, my love, don't you look smashing. I thought
you'd be in Tangiers shooting the summer fashions for
Vogue.

IAN: I'll let my assistants shoot Twiggy in swimsuits. A bloody bore it all is. Has Fauna arrived yet?

ANTHEA: Indeed. You can find her at the end of the bar in deep conversation with a young garment industry mogul from New York. Oh look, Julie Christie has arrived. And there's Mick and Marianne and Keith and Anita. Mick! Mick! I adored the record. Thank you! "Street Fighting Man" will be your biggest hit yet! *(To* IAN*)* Of course, my husband wants to melt it down for moustache wax. Bootsie's such an old fart. There's the Shrimp! I'm so pleased that Rose and Jean Shrimpton are chums and not rivals, but then that is the spirit of the times. Make love not war, *n'est-ce pas?* John Lennon looks quite the worse for wear. Tell me darling, do you think it's true the Beatles are splitting up?

IAN *(drunk and weary of* ANTHEA*'s chatter):* I haven't given it much thought, Anthea.

ANTHEA: I see the party began for you quite a bit earlier.

IAN: Several days earlier in fact.

(FAUNA *enters in one of her own dazzling creations accompanied by* BARRY POSNER, *a young New York fashion industry mogul)*

FAUNA *(to* IAN*):* There you are, darling. My dear, Mr. Barry Posner is dying to meet you. This young man practically runs New York's rag trade.

BARRY: Man, I really go apeshit over your work. They're not just fashion photos, but like statements about sensuality.

IAN *(pulling her downstage right):* Fauna, I need to talk to you.

FAUNA: Can't it wait, darling?

IAN: Do you have any uppers?

FAUNA *(annoyed):* I can't believe you are asking me this now. *(She rejoins the others)*

BARRY: So where's the legendary Briar Rose? Isn't this her shindig?

ANTHEA: Leave it to Briar Rose to make a grand entrance at her own party.

BARRY: Fauna, honey, I am not leaving this affair without your signature. You don't know me. I'm the boy wonder of Seventh Avenue. I know from marketing. Believe me, I can do.

IAN: Believe him, he can do. Now give me some of your lovely black beauties.

FAUNA *(to* ANTHEA*):* Barry wants to market a fashion line for me in the states.

IAN: You're ignoring me Fauna, I don't like it.

FAUNA: I ignore little boys when they're naughty. *(She shoots* IAN *a withering look)*

ANTHEA: But your clothes are already in the finest stores in the U.S. I've seen them.

BARRY: This is something different. These are clothes for the youth market. All synthetic and at bargain prices. And the little lady doesn't have to do bupkis. My people will design the garments. All you do is enjoy.

ANTHEA *(looking offstage):* Oh dear, look what just walked in.

IAN: Sebastian Loré.

FAUNA: I thought you said she was dead.

IAN: That was her sister, the wicked witch of the East. She's worse than the other one was.

FAUNA: And he must be spitting bullets that his collection was such a flop.

ANTHEA: Well my dear, an entire collection of tissue paper evening gowns was bound to be a mistake.

FAUNA: He was desperately trying to be with it.

(SEBASTIAN *enters in the height of outlandish mod fasion*)

SEBASTIAN: My precious darlings. Anthea, it's been ages.

ANTHEA: Good evening, Sebastian. I do hope you've come here in the spirit of friendship.

SEBASTIAN: Friendship of the purest nature. My dearest darling Fauna. *(Kisses her)* Now Mr. McKenzie, you may kiss me. Don't be afraid. Think of me as you would a kindly old aunt. *(They kiss)*

FAUNA: Sebastian, this is Barry Posner. Sebastian Loré.

BARRY: Are you in the industry?

SEBASTIAN *(laughs):* On the fringe, dear boy. But where is our lovely Rose, our Briar Rose?

ANTHEA: I wonder what could be keeping her.

(BRIAR ROSE [ENID] *enters in the wildest outfit and coiffure of all*)

SEBASTIAN: Ah, the goddess emerges.

ANTHEA: Happy birthday, darling.

ENID: Thank you so much for throwing this party.

FAUNA: Darling. You look lovely. *(They kiss)*

IAN: Hello, luv.

SEBASTIAN: Remember me?

ENID *(startled):* Mr. Loré . . .

SEBASTIAN: Don't say a word. All of our problems are in the past. I come only to celebrate you.

ENID: You don't despise me for walking out on you?

SEBASTIAN: How can I despise someone for grabbing a better opportunity. I would have done the same thing meself at a younger age. As a matter of fact, I'd like to make a toast to the modern Aphrodite—

ANTHEA *(with wild enthusiasm, sees someone out front):* Could it be? It couldn't. It is! It's Garbo!

EVERYONE: Garbo!

(FAUNA, IAN, SEBASTIAN *and* BARRY *join* ANTHEA *to gaze upon Garbo.* ENID *looks at her from stage left. Unseen by all,* MISS THICK, SEBASTIAN's *secretary, tiptoes out carrying a black box marked LSD. Without* ENID *noticing,* MISS THICK *pours some of the LSD into the drink in* ENID's *outstretched hand and scurries off)*

ANTHEA *(seeing it's not Garbo):* Well, it looked like her. *(The group moans in disappointment)*

SEBASTIAN: As I was saying. A toast to the incomparable Briar Rose.

EVERYONE: Cheers! *(They all drink)*

FAUNA *(to* ENID): Darling, I heard all about the Schlesinger film. You're really switched on.

BARRY: Excuse me for interrupting, but I'm not giving up. Fauna, name your price and then how's about dancing with me.

FAUNA: Name my price? That's more like it, boy wonder. Let's dance. *(They do a strenuous dance number and everyone joins in. At the end of the number,* ENID *begins to feel the effect of the LSD and screams)*

ENID *(stares at* FAUNA): Fauna, you face is turning into the most peculiar pattern of paisley.

FAUNA: The lighting is rather grim but . . .

ENID: What's wrong with your nose? It keeps growing longer. Get it away from me before you sneeze.

ANTHEA: Is this a new lingo?

IAN: Luv, are you all right?

ENID: I don't know. I feel like I'm on a rollercoaster that's flying off the track. Coo, Mick Jagger's lips are getting so huge. I bet I could bounce off them like a trampoline.

SEBASTIAN: I think the dear girl's drunk too much.

IAN: It's not alcohol. She's tripping on LSD!

SEBASTIAN: Perhaps we should get her home.

ENID *(to* SEBASTIAN): It's the wicked witch! Get her away from me! She turns young girls into department store manne- quins. Get her away from me!

SEBASTIAN: She's quite fanciful, isn't she? Come, dear.

ENID: No, I'm not going with you! I know what you want. I won't do it! I won't let you drain my life away! Get away! Get away from me! *(She sinks to the floor)*

FAUNA *(frantic):* Oh my God, she's unconscious.

IAN: I've never seen this happen before.

FAUNA *(holding* ENID): Quick, someone call a doctor. Anthea, hurry!

(ANTHEA *screams in panic. Blackout)*

IAN *(back at the pub):* She never woke up. The doctors said it was a strange mixture of LSD that induced the coma. In effect, Fauna and I slipped into the coma with her that night. I haven't shot another photograph. Fauna sold everything and went into seclusion. Dammit, don't you realize the sixties are over!

(The giant eyes of the fashion drawing on the backdrop close. Blackout.)

Scene Nine

The present. CRAIG PRINCE, *a handsome young nutritionist, is being interviewed by a health magazine.*

CRAIG: What's the name of your magazine? "Natural High?" Of course, I'm sorry. This book tour has been amazing. A different city every day, radio shows, newspaper interviews. I'm not complaining. Only two years ago people thought I was a nut harping on these wierd theories about vitamins and nutrition. I guess 1986 is my year. Basically I'm blown away that there's been so much media attention to my book, "Eating Right is the Best Revenge." I know what you want me to talk about so I'll get that over with first. I'll just start at the beginning again. I came to London in June 1984. A good friend of mine, Clive, was ill and I went to visit him at a small sanitarium. It was a creepy place. It looked like an old castle, probably was one at one time. Well, I have one lousy sense of direction and I must have turned the wrong corner and I found myself in a completely different wing. Very still and very empty. I looked around for a nurse or anyone to help

me find my way out. At the end of the corridor was an open
door and a strange figure in black. I assumed it was a nun.

(Flashback. FAUNA, *garbed in a black cape and hat with a veil,
brings on the comatose* ENID *in a wheelchair)*

CRAIG: Excuse me.

FAUNA *(taken by surprise):* Who are you?

CRAIG: I'm sorry, I thought you were someone else.

FAUNA: How did you get in here?

CRAIG: I'm lost. This place is like a maze.

FAUNA: Please go.

CRAIG: Who is she? She's so beautiful.

FAUNA: Enid Wetwhistle.

CRAIG: I've seen that face before. What happened to her?

FAUNA: A bad acid trip. She's been in a coma for fifteen years.

CRAIG: I'm a nutritionist. I can tell many things about a person
merely be pressing certain vitamins in their hands. I can
instantly tell what elements their system is lacking. (CRAIG
takes vitamins out of his pocket and presses them in ENID*'s
hand)* She could use some super Bs. As well as a good dose of
D and E. Lecithin would help and Lysine and some pure
bioflavonoids. You'll probably think I'm a nutcase, but I've
been experimenting with llama enzymes and that might just
do it for her. Let me work on this. (FAUNA *exits. Again, in the
present)* Well, I did. I worked hard. I was obsessed by that
silent face. I returned the following week and when the
doctors and nurses weren't looking, I injected her with a
megadose of fifty-eight different vitamin and mineral combi-

nations, as well as some high density llama enzymes. *(In the past)* Oh Sleeping Beauty, will nothing disturb your eternal slumber? *(He injects her and kisses her. She awakes. The eyes on the backdrop open as well)*

ENID: Where are the Beatles? I heard all four of them were coming to the party.

CRAIG: That party's over. A new one's about to begin.

ENID: Who are you?

CRAIG: Craig Prince. What's your name?

ENID: Briar Rose . . . No, Enid Wetwhistle . . . No, Briar Rose. Briar Rose and Enid Wetwhistle. I suppose they're one and the same. How very strange and sort of wonderful. I think I'd like to stretch my legs. I must say, I've certainly had a good night's sleep. *(She exits)*

CRAIG *(in the present):* With Briar Rose restored to life, I then brought back to life her two friends, Ian McKenzie and Fauna Alexander, two leading figures of the swinging sixties. I converted them all to my philosophy of nutrition and enzyme action and now they're all on tour with me plugging my book and video tapes.

(IAN enters dressed in the height of new wave fashion)

IAN: Yup, we're all on the comeback trail. Craig made me realize that my drug and drinking habits were largely due to a severe case of hypoglycemia. For the first time in years, I can really see clearly. I've just shot the entire December issue of Vogue and I'm about to start directing a big budget music video starring none other than Briar Rose and costumed by Fauna Alexander.

(FAUNA enters dressed in the epitome of outrageous contemporary chic)

FAUNA: Ian is right. We owe so much to Craig and his llamas with their miracle enzymes. For the first time I'm not ashamed to admit that, for many years, I was suffering from anorexia bulemia. Craig has cured me of that terrifying disease. I'm also developing a new perfume with a llama base as well as opening four "Fauna's Boutiques" in New York, Los Angeles, Tokyo and Palm Springs. We've regained the spirit of youth.

(ENID *enters. She too is costumed in the high fashion style of today*)

ENID: And then of course, I'd still be fast asleep if it wasn't for Craig. He's bringing me to Ho-Ho-Kus, New Jersey next week to meet his mum.

CRAIG: Shall we tell them the happy news?

ENID: Craig and I are going to be married.

FAUNA: I also have some important news. I'm going to have a baby.

IAN: And I'm the lucky dad.

ENID: My dear friends, I'm so happy for you.

FAUNA: And I'm so happy for you.

IAN: I'm happy, too.

CRAIG: So am I. I guess we have it all.

(SEBASTIAN *and* MISS THICK *enter in dirty rags*)

SEBASTIAN: You may wonder what became of Sebastian Loré and Miss Thick. We punished ourselves with our own guilt. And so we emigrated to Guatemala where we pick papayas to feed the poor. Only last week, I unearthed a tattered copy of People magazine and there I read that Rose and Craig and Fauna and Ian were all living quite happily ever after.

(The two romantic couples are holding hands. IAN *turns to look at* CRAIG *and they wink. They go back to their gals and kiss. The lights blackout. The lights flash on again rather like a photographer's flashbulb catching the couples in amused surprise. Blackout.)*

THE END

Madeleine Astarte (Carole Monferdini, at left) and La Condesa (David Drake, center) put their centuries-old rivalry on hold for the benefit of gossip columnist, Oatsie Carewe (Roy Cockrum).

Photo by T.L Boston

VAMPIRE LESBIANS OF SODOM

PROLOGUE

Sodom in days of old. Two GUARDS *are standing sentry before the entrance to a forbidding cave.*

ALI: Who goes there?

HUJAR: You needn't fear Ali. No one ventures near this spot save for madmen and fools.

ALI: Including you and me.

HUJAR: Yes, but we are clever fools. For our deed today, we shall receive a kingly sum.

ALI: If we live to spend it.

HUJAR: The creature we guard desires nothing of the likes of you. The Succubus thrives upon the blood of young virgins.

ALI: A rare delicacy, eh?

HUJAR: You must be new to these parts. Where do your people hail from?

ALI: I hail from Ishbar, in Asia Minor. You know, the fertile crescent.

HUJAR: So what brings you to Sodom?

ALI: Don't scoff, but I've come to seek my fortune.

HUJAR: Then my friend, you've made a wise move. This city has everything. It never sleeps. Have you been to the bars?

ALI: No, I'm living out in Gommorah.

HUJAR: Gommorah?

ALI: Hujar, I don't want to offend you, but I'm really not into bars. I'm looking for a relationship.

HUJAR: Then my man, you shouldn't have moved to the twin cities. *(A cock crows)* The cock has crowed. It's time to begin. The Succubus demands its breakfast.

ALI: Have you ever seen the Succubus?

HUJAR: No one has, except for the virgin sacrifice and, obviously, they never live to tell. We had best begin. The sleeping potion will wear off, the virgin will awake and we'll have a lot of explaining to do. You wait here. I'll bring her in. *(He exits.* HUJAR *returns carrying in his arms the beautiful young virgin)* Quite a beauty, isn't she? A pity she is to be sacrificed.

ALI: Hujar, she stirs.

HUJAR: That cannot be. The potion should last an hour more. Damn the gods, let's get out of here. *(The* GIRL *begins to wake in his arms)*

GIRL: No, Papa, I don't want to play. Please, don't make me. *(She awakes)* Where am I? Who are you? Please sir, release me. *(He puts her on her feet. The virgin is indeed beautiful, but there is something about her costume and demeanor that suggests a stripper performing a burlesque sketch about vestal virgins. It could be the G-string and spike heels)*

HUJAR: We are soldiers under the command of the Governor.

GIRL: My mind is such a jumble. I had such a strange dream. I dreamt there was a lottery to choose a sacrificial victim for the dreaded Succubus and I dreamed that I chose the black stone of death. You know, they say our dreams can be interpreted. They can tell us many things about ourselves. I wonder what this dream means.

HUJAR: That was no dream, that was the truth. You are the virgin sacrifice.

GIRL *(thinks they're joking):* You couldn't be . . . but surely you . . . no, I . . . I couldn't . . . It's imposs . . . *(She realizes it's true and screams.* HUJAR *grabs her around the neck)*

HUJAR: Another peep out of you and we'll rip your tongue out.

ALI: Hujar, be kind to the girl. These are her last moments on earth.

HUJAR: And they shall be ours if her screams bring forth the Succubus. (ALI *breaks* HUJAR's *arm away)*

GIRL: Please sir, I beg of you. If there is any shred of pity or tenderness in your heart. Please, do not deliver me to the Succubus.

HUJAR: We only follow our orders.

GIRL *(to* ALI): You, you have the eyes of a poet. Surely you cannot see it just to send me to this most horrible of deaths.

ALI: I wish there was something I could do.

HUJAR: Soldier, control yourself. You are acting weak and womanish.

GIRL: If having a kind heart is womanish, be proud of your womanhood. I implore you, sir, save me. My father has money. Aid my escape and all of his gold shall be yours.

HUJAR: Child, you have been forsaken. Your father has publicly announced his pride in your selection as food for the goddess.

GIRL: I refuse to believe this.

ALI: It's true. We have his sworn testimonial of acceptance.

GIRL: Then it is true. I am truly alone. A mere child of fourteen. Friendless, parentless, damned to this most vile fate. Tell me, my good executioners, how much time do I have?

HUJAR: But a few minutes more.

GIRL: Then permit me a moment whilst I bid farewell to my girlhood. *(In a reverie)* Goodbye youth. Adieu bubbling brook of joy, rosy hope of budding romance. I bid farewell to the frothy games of catching a whip'o'whill and skipping to its tune, lightning bugs parading their brilliance before the first evening stars. I wave goodbye to the beardless boys who breathlessly snatched a forbidden kiss and the silly girls who giggled at my follies. Goodbye dear friends. Farewell round orb.

ALI: Is there nothing I can do to ease your pain?

GIRL: Yes, there is something you could do. Break my hymen. Rape me and I'll no longer be a virgin fit for sacrifice.

ALI: But, I. . . . *(The* GIRL *rips off* ALI's *loincloth and chases him around screaming, "Break my hymen, break my hymen!"* HUJAR *pushes her to the ground)*

HUJAR: The child is mad. Away! *(The two soldiers exit)*

GIRL: I beseech thee, Isis, provide me with the courage to face my destruction.

(The SUCCUBUS *enters in the form of a beautiful and very hard–boiled dame. She is by turns very grand and also a bit cheap but, most importantly, she has a very big chip on her shoulder)*

GIRL: Run! Save yourself! The creature is about to emerge.

SUCCUBUS *(irritated):* Hey, hey, hey! Where are you going?

GIRL: Woman, have you lost your senses?

SUCCUBUS: Not that I'm aware of.

GIRL: Who are you?

SUCCUBUS: Give a guess.

GIRL: An actress?

SUCCUBUS: Guess again.

GIRL: Are you a courtesan?

SUCCUBUS: I am the Succubus that you've heard tell about.

GIRL: How can pure evil be embodied by such beauty?

SUCCUBUS: How much easier to lure you into my arms. Come, child.

GIRL: Vile thing, what right have you to demand my death?

SUCCUBUS *(angrily):* Do I not also have the right to life? As you need food and water so I need the pure unsullied blood of virgins.

GIRL: What proof have you of my maidenhead? What if I told you I was the village slut, a repository for every man's seed in Sodom?

SUCCUBUS: I'd say you were a big fat liar. Now you tax my patience, child. Come.

GIRL: I'm afraid to die.

SUCCUBUS *(with great self pity):* That's nothing to be afraid of. Think how much crueler my fate, never to die, condemned to immortality. The perennial witness to the eternal passing parade. My cave is quite the lonely one.

GIRL: Forgive me if I don't weep.

SUCCUBUS: A spitfire, eh? But why should you pity me? I suppose you look at me now and imagine I'm quite a glamorous, flamboyant creature. In your ignorance, you fancy my life to be one of extravagance and magic. How wrong you are. Yes, I have my slaves that do my bidding, but they are semi-human primitive creatures and far from scintillating dinner companions. True, my cave is overflowing with sparkling jewels, but where the fuck can I wear them? My life stinks. The only enjoyment I get is a vestal virgin now and then. But time goes on and I survive and how? How you may wonder do I face the prospect of a millenium of time on my hands? What keeps me going is a sense of humor. I look for small inconsequential things that will provide me with amusement and so

far, in that department, my fair young lady, you're not rack-
ing up any gutbusters.

GIRL: You play at human feelings, but you possess as much
humanity as the dragons at sea.

SUCCUBUS: Child, I must say I am impressed by your fortitude.
If you were a fellow Succubus, I might even be afraid of you.
But you are not. You will look into my eyes and all thought of
defiance shall vanish. Look into my eyes. Look into my eyes.
Look into my eyes! *(The* GIRL *is hypnotized by the* SUCCU-
BUS) You will come to me now. *(Very imperiously and most
unseductively)* Seek out my warmth. Suckle at my breast.

GIRL *(crosses to the* SUCCUBUS): Yes, yes, protect me, dear
mother. *(The* SUCCUBUS *lunges toward the* GIRL *and drinks
her blood ravenously. Blackout.)*

Scene Two

Hollywood, 1920. The drawing room of LA CONDESA*'s spectacular mansion high in the Hollywood hills.* KING CARLISLE, *a handsome young matinee idol, is pacing back and forth.* ETIENNE, LA CONDESA*'s extremely nervous butler, enters.*

ETIENNE: Young man, you will have to leave at once. Madame La Condesa is incommunicado.

KING: You have kept me waiting for over an hour. I demand to see La Condesa. Why won't she see me?

ETIENNE: Madame is ruled by her caprices.

KING: This is intolerable. Sir, don't you know who I am?

ETIENNE: Are you here to fix the victrola?

KING: I take it you never go to the movies.

ETIENNE: I only see Madame's films.

KING: I am King Carlisle, the newest and biggest male star in silent pictures. She can't treat me this way.

ETIENNE: My good man, only yesterday Madame received Winston Churchill, Monsieur Diaghilev and the King of Spain. King Carlisle? Small potatoes.

KING: Well, Monsieur Le Butler, I consider your mistress even smaller potatoes. Furthermore, I am not impressed by her phoney title, Madame La Condesa Scrofula de Hoya, indeed. Surely she knows that the studio has brought the great stage actress, Madeleine Astarté, out to Hollywood and is grooming her as Magda's rival.

ETIENNE: Magda Legerdemain is a great artist with the divine spark. Madeleine Astarté: pure hambone.

KING: You must help me. I have nothing against your mistress. I merely wish to save my fiancée Renee from her clutches. Renee is an innocent. She is new to Hollywood. She doesn't recognize corruption when she sees it. I must save her from La Condesa.

ETIENNE: What have you to fear?

KING: There are so many rumors surrounding Magda Legerdemain. Rumors that she's not only a vamp but . . . a vampire.

ETIENNE: Excuse me, I must go. It's time to run Madame's leopards in Griffith Park. (*He tries to leave.* KING *stops him*)

KING: You're hiding something from me.

ETIENNE (*screams*): Don't touch me! I will tell you this. You have entered a mad household. This isn't hair on my head, these are nerve endings.

KING: Then why do you work here?

ETIENNE: Who else but Madame would employ me? You don't recognize me, do you?

KING: No, who are you?

ETIENNE: Suffering has changed my face as completely as a surgeon's scalpel. I will tell you this. Baby Kelly Ambrose lives!

KING: Surely you're not Baby Kelly Ambrose, the hatchet wielding vaudeville child star.

ETIENNE *(breaks into a timestep and swings an imaginary hatchet):* I did them all in after a milk fund benefit in Kokomo. I dismembered all six of them and scattered their body parts along the entire Keith-Orpheum circuit. Only one person would aid my escape from the lunatic asylum and that was La Condesa and, for her sake, I would gladly strike again.

KING: Oh dear, I must remove Renee from this bedlam.

(RENEE VAIN *runs on and speaks to* ETIENNE. RENEE *is a lovely ingenue in the Mary Pickford mode but with the toughness of a Ma Barker)*

RENEE: Etienne, La Condesa would like . . . *(sees* KING) King, what on earth are you doing here?

KING: My dearest darling, I'm here to talk some sense into you.

RENEE: Please, go away. You don't understand.

KING: I understand all too well.

RENEE *(with mad vitality):* No, you don't. You want me to lead a quiet, dreary life as your wife. Well, that's not why I came to Hollywood. I want to live! I want to drive my roadster faster than anyone else on the road. I want to stay up all night, drinking whiskey and dancing on table tops. *(Laughs with wild abandon)* I'm young, let me be reckless!

KING: My darling, I fear for you.

RENEE: Etienne, could you leave us alone for a moment?

ETIENNE: If you think that's wise. *(He exits)*

RENEE *(as tough as nails):* King, you nincompoop, you're going to spoil everything. This dame's my entree to the big wigs in this burg. She knows everyone. We had breakfast with Wallace Reid, lunch with Alma Rubens, tea with Clare Kimball Young and dinner with Rod La Rocque. This place is a social gold mine and I'm reaping in the nuggets. I got me three screen tests lined up for next week.

KING: But I know people. I could help you.

RENEE *(disdainfully):* Oh, a lot of help you are. You got me tossed off the DeMille picture. You didn't think I knew that, did you?

KING: The role was cheap and degrading.

RENEE: Let me be cheap and degraded, I'm an actress! I've had enough of you butting into my career, you great big buddinsky! *(He reaches for her)* Don't touch me. You repulse me. When I think of your feeble attempts to make love to me, I laugh. Do you hear me, I laugh. *(Explodes in hysterical laughter)*

KING *(shakes her violently):* Stop it! Stop it! This isn't you, this isn't my Renee.

RENEE *(suddenly lovely and vulnerable):* King, I don't know what came over me. That was a different girl speaking. Some strange power overtook me and made me say those cruel words. Can you forgive me?

KING: Of course, darling. I must get you out of this mansion. Can't you smell the presence of evil?

(LA CONDESA [*la* CONDAYSA] *enters garbed in the barbaric excesses of silent screen vamps. She is of course the* SUCCUBUS *from Sodom looking not a day older*)

LA CONDESA: Mr. Carlisle, you smell the presence of evil? Perhaps you are mistaking it for my perfume. If you are, it's expensive evil, fifty dollars an ounce. Now state your business.

KING: I demand that you give up Renee.

LA CONDESA (*with flamboyant levity*): Give her up? I see no handcuffs, I see no chains.

KING: I believe she is under your spell. I've heard tales of the stream of young girls who pass through these portals. Young starlets who are never heard of again. Where are those starlets?

LA CONDESA (*very grandly*): If you must know, I give them private coaching. I audition them and I give them an honest appraisal of their talent. Can I help it if they all go back to Wichita?

RENEE: Tonight she's going to teach me how to play a passionate love scene.

KING: I can't bear this torment. Don't you know what she is?

RENEE: A very nice lady.

KING (*with self righteous fury*): This very nice lady drinks the blood of young virgins. Yes, I know the truth about you, Madame La Condesa. I know you had to flee Europe because of the rumors of your evil ways. And here you are corrupting every virgin in Hollywood.

LA CONDESA: Slim pickings, I must say. If I were interested in virgins, why the hell would I come to Hollywood? My friend, you've seen too many motion pictures.

KING: I am not your friend. I spit on your friendship! *(He spits on the floor)*

LA CONDESA *(mad as a hornet)*: Spit on my friendship, but not on my rug!

KING: I will, I will if that will save my Renee. *(Spits several times)*

LA CONDESA *(with great vulgarity)*: You clam up one more time and there's gonna be hell to pay. Etienne! Clean up this mess. (ETIENNE *runs in*) Now look here you . . .

ETIENNE: Madame, Miss Carewe from the Hearst newspapers will be here momentarily. Don't you think you should be composing yourself?

LA CONDESA: Yes, I must compose myself before that nosy bitch arrives. Mr. Carlisle, the door is that way.

KING: I am not leaving. I shall be here when Oatsie Carewe arrives and I shall provide her with some juicy gossip for her column.

RENEE *(angrily)*: You wouldn't!

ETIENNE: Madame, shall I call the police?

LA CONDESA: No, let him stay. And let him repeat this slander. It shall only add fuel to my legend.

(Doorbell rings)

LA CONDESA: That must be Miss Carewe. Show her in, Etienne. (ETIENNE *exits*)

RENEE: King, I wish you would get the point that you're not wanted here. (ETIENNE *enters*)

ETIENNE: Madame Madeleine Astarté.

LA CONDESA *(aghast):* Astarté!

RENEE: What's she doing here?

LA CONDESA: Tell her to go away. Tell her I'm not receiving.

(MADELEINE ASTARTÉ [ASTARTAY] *enters in the grand manner. She is none other than the virgin from Sodom, now the dazzling grande dame of the New York stage)*

MADELEINE: Balderdash, La Condesa. I've traveled all the way from New York just to see you.

LA CONDESA: You must not flatter me. All Hollywood knows of your million–dollar contract.

MADELEINE *(with gaiety):* Million point five. The point five, darlings, is to keep me in mascara. *(Laughs and looks at* ETIENNE *next to her. She does a big burlesque double take at his deadpan expression)*

LA CONDESA: Madame Astarté, I would love to offer you tea, but unfortunately I'm expecting Oatsie Carewe any minute for an in–depth profile.

MADELEINE: Oh, I must stay for that. I do so want to get to know you better. Besides this will dispel all those awful rumors that we're rivals. How absurd, you and I rivals. We couldn't possibly play the same roles. Perhaps mother and daughter.

LA CONDESA *(lightly bitchy):* Dear, you look entirely too young to play my mother.

MADELEINE: Aren't you kind, Contessa.

LA CONDESA *(cordially correcting her.):* Condesa (CONDAYSA). Madeleine, if I may be so familiar, have they chosen your first vehicle?

MADELEINE: Yes, I'm to do the life of Madame DuBarry.

LA CONDESA: This is an outrage! I am to play DuBarry. My costumes are all made.

MADELEINE: We had to take in the waist a little. Lay off the paté, Cunt-tessa.

LA CONDESA *(angrily):* Condesa! (CONDAYSA)

MADELEINE: After the DuBarry picture I shall do the life of Mary Magdalene.

LA CONDESA: You little bitch, that was supposed to be my follow-up picture.

MADELEINE: Dear heart, I do hope you won't mind, but the studio felt they needed a real actress for the role.

LA CONDESA: This is sheer treachery and you won't get away with this! *(Turns to leave)*

KING: Madame Astarté, she has the devil on her side.

LA CONDESA: I'll fix you, I'll fix you by all the powers that be!

RENEE: What will you do?

LA CONDESA *(with intense frustration):* I'm calling my agent! *(She exits)*

ETIENNE: Oh dear! *(Follows her out)*

KING: Madeleine, I fear for your life. You may think me mad, but I have reason to believe La Condesa is one of the undead.

MADELEINE: No darling, she just looks like death. *(To* RENEE*)* But you, my dear, you look much livelier. I don't believe we've met.

RENEE: My name is Renee Vain. I'm a new contract player at the studio.

MADELEINE: How perfectly divine. You have such a lovely face. Profile. Ah, yes.

KING: We're engaged to be married.

MADELEINE: Pish posh. An actress must be married to her art. Men, ugh. *(Shudders)* Thespis shall be your lover.

RENEE: That's what La Condesa says.

MADELEINE: Does she? I suppose you and La Condesa are quite intimate.

RENEE: I love her so much.

MADELEINE: Yes, an older woman can be such a comfort to a young girl. I can tell you are a superb actress and we must play together. I know the perfect vehicle. I've just optioned a new book on an old subject. The story of Sapho. I play Sapho, a noble Greek woman, passionate, vibrant, a sexual revolutionary and you, my fair one, you shall play her lesbian lover . . . *(Searches for a name)* Rusty.

RENEE: Rusty?

MADELEINE: I can see the scene. The cameraman lining up the shot. The director calls "Action," the off screen violinist commences to play. Sapho sees Rusty coming out of the Parthenon, the wind tossing her hair away from her face.

Sapho slips her arm around Rusty's waist and silently they . . .

RENEE: But I don't . . .

MADELEINE: I said silently, they walk down a dark winding street. It's the street where Sapho lives with her grandmother, Ruchel. The street is empty, everyone being at the Olympic games. They look into each other's eyes. Rusty finds herself yielding to the older woman's incandescent beauty. Cameras pan in for a tight shot. They kiss. *(They kiss and then* ASTARTÉ *bites* RENEE*'s neck until the girl faints)* Kill the lights, call it a wrap.

KING *(in shock):* You . . . you . . . you're a vampire!

MADELEINE: I don't suppose you have a handkerchief.

KING: She devil! Fiend! You've killed my Renee.

MADELEINE: Nah, she'll come to, but let's say I've taken the bloom off the peach.

KING: I'll expose you, I'll expose you as the monster you are.

MADELEINE *(coolly):* I wouldn't talk about exposing anyone if I were you.

KING: What do you mean?

MADELEINE: I happen to know King Carlisle's not your real name.

KING: So, many stars change their names.

MADELEINE: I happen to know your real name is Trixie Monahan and before you came to Hollywood, you worked as what is politely called a model/escort with a strictly male clientele. Trixie Monahan, I'll expose you as a homosexual.

KING *(dissolving into tears):* Yes, it's true, it's true. I am, I am.

MADELEINE: You may one day marry and even have children but you will always be a homosexual. *(With monstrous ferocity)* ALWAYS!

KING: Then there's nothing left for me to do but kill myself.

MADELEINE: There are other alternatives.

KING: Such as?

MADELEINE: You can be my personal slave.

KING: What would you expect of me?

MADELEINE: Lots of things. Escort me to premieres, wash my car, rinse out my dirty panties, but don't you dare let me catch you wearing them. I get plenty mad.

(He collapses into despair. LA CONDESA *enters)*

LA CONDESA: What is this? What have you done to her? Now you've really gone too far. You imagine yourself quite the cunning vixen. You have delusions that you can conquer me. Though I have always found you vulgar, I have never taken you for a fool, until now. Hollywood is my town. For centuries, you have been an albatross around my neck. First in Rome, I claimed as my bride the most beautiful of Caligula's courtesans. She was mine until you stole her away to China. Then there was the nun in the dark ages who became my personal slave, stolen once again. We all know what treachery you conspired against me during the Spanish Inquisition, but I triumphed. And did I plot revenge? No. Then in the sixteenth century, I had as my mistress the most desired of Queen Elizabeth's ladies in waiting. You, the everpresent vulture, snatched her off to the colonies. Even then, did I choose revenge? No. And why? Because I am a great lady. I conduct myself with dignity and grandeur whilst you roll in

the gutter, parading your twat onstage and calling it acting.
You've got as much glamour as a common street whore and
now, madame, you have gone too far. I am the queen of
vampires and I shall never, never relinquish my hold on
Hollywood!

MADELEINE: Are you through? As you desire to relive the past,
shall we travel even further back in time? Many centuries
ago, back in the days of the Bible, there was a young girl, a
mere child of fourteen, a lovely girl, full of high spirits. A
lottery was held to choose a sacrificial victim for the dreaded
Succubus. As fate would have it, she chose the black stone of
death. She was dragged by soldiers to the cave of the creature and there left to her desecration. The monster emerged
and there under a godless sky, the creature dug her teeth
into the girl's fair flesh. Having gorged itself, the monster
retired to its cave, leaving the girl's body to be pecked and
devoured as carrion. But the girl did not die. The monster in
its fury did not even notice that all the while it was sucking
the girl's blood, the child herself had lodged her teeth into a
vein of the monster. In her terror she drank. More and more
she filled herself with the creature's fluid. And there on that
bleached rocky point, left to rot like a piece of old meat, the
girl did not die but was transformed, transformed into one of
the undead, never to find eternal rest, but to stalk the earth
forever in search of a victim, forever alone, forever damned.
Look at me, I am that girl! And I demand the death of the
Succubus!

(ETIENNE *enters*)

ETIENNE: Miss Oatsie Carewe of the Hearst Newspapers.

(OATSIE CAREWE *enters*)

OATSIE: Darling! And Madeleine Astarté, too. What a marvelous surprise. Who'd have thought you two gals would be
chums. And they say Hollywood is a heartless town. Magda, I
adore the dress. It does wonders for your figure, so conceal-

ing. And Madeleine, I just know that must be a Paris creation. I must have a description of it for my column.

LA CONDESA: Oatsie darling, may I get you some tea?

OATSIE: No, no, never touch the stuff. Okay girls, straight from the hip, how did this feud rumor begin?

LA CONDESA: What feud? I adore Madeleine. I've adored her for what seems like centuries.

OATSIE (*sees* KING *and* RENEE): What's this? King Carlisle, Renee Vain, two stars of tomorrow.

MADELEINE: Do you know, this wonderful lady spends her free time coaching young actors. They were just performing a scene for us and are totally exhausted. Such is the dramatic art.

LA CONDESA: Oh yes, she knows. It's not all glamour.

MADELEINE: So true, so true. Particularly when you act, Magda. Such shattering realism. Why, you're more than realistic, you're nearly grotesque.

LA CONDESA: Thank you, dear.

OATSIE: Madeleine, I want to give you a real Hollywood welcome. I just insist you come to my house for dinner. I'm a demon in the kitchen and you come too, Magda, I insist. What shall I make? A goulash. Yes, a nice thick goulash, a native dish of Transylvania. Have you ever been there, Magda?

LA CONDESA: No, I don't believe I've ever been to Transylvania. No doubt Madeline has been there on one of her theatrical tours.

MADELEINE: No, I've never played Transylvania. Altoona, yes, Transylvania, no.

OATSIE: I adore a good goulash, spiced with plenty of garlic. I hope you don't have an aversion to garlic.

LA CONDESA: No, no, the hotter the better. Remember, I was once married to a Spanish nobleman, the Count Scrofula de Hoya. *(With a heavy Castilian lisp)* We lived in Barthelona, a thity renowned for its thpithy cuithine.

MADELEINE: Ah Thpain. The bullfights, the flamenco dancers.

OATSIE: And the magnificent cathedrals. One of my great passions is collecting models of the crucifixion. *(She takes out a cross)* This, Condesa, is a Florentine cross, blessed by the brothers of Santa Giovanna. *(The two vampires recoil and twitch with frenzy.* RENEE *awakes)*

KING: Ah Renee, my precious.

RENEE: I must have been dreaming. I dreamt I was being devoured by a horrid black bat. *(Sees* MADELEINE *and screams)* It was you, it was you!

MADELEINE: Can't you shut her up?

OATSIE: You can't shut out the truth.

MADELEINE: What the . . . *(She turns to* OATSIE. OATSIE *flashes the cross at her, causing* MADELEINE'*s hips to bump like a burlesque stripper)*

OATSIE: I've studied your evil legends all my life. I know you both very well, but you don't know me. Let me introduce myself. *(She flings her coat open and throws it to the floor, revealing a man's military jacket covered with medals and polkadotted boxer shorts. She throws off her hat and wig, uncovering a shining bald pate. In a thick German dialect)* I am Gregory Salazar, vampire hunter! God in all of his mercy has cast me in the role of avenging angel to rid the world of your filth.

LA CONDESA: You silly little man, you have no power over us. You shall long be dust while we are forever young. *(He shows her the cross and she too begins to twitch wildly)*

SALAZAR: At this very moment, the Los Angeles police are surrounding this mansion. The fire department is spraying the walls with holy water. We've got you cornered. Daughters of Lucifer, your reign of death is over. We shall hold you both in this room until the sun rises, the sun which will transform you both into ancient hags and then decaying skeletons and then dust. I will sweep the dust into the gutter with the rest of the swill. From there your remains will float down the pipes into the public sewer where no one will know the difference between your ashes and the rest of the waste products of the Greater Los Angeles Area.

MADELEINE: La Condesa, have you the power to evoke the cry of the banshee?

LA CONDESA: I know the ritual, but I've never achieved it.

SALAZAR: You do not frighten us with your primitive black magic.

LA CONDESA and MADELEINE:
Flee from Hades, spirits rare.
We free you from your devil's lair,
Paint our victims a deep blood red,
Banshees, phantoms, vampires dead.

SALAZAR: Breathe your last, Brides of Beelzebub!

LA CONDESA and MADELEINE:
Far, far into the night
Remove this enemy from our sight

Burn his flesh till it's black with char,
The vampire killer, Salazar!

(SALAZAR's *face grows grotesque as he writhes in agony*)

KING: Look at his face!

MADELEINE: Flee, Sister, flee! *(The two vampiresses exit as* RENEE *unleashes a bloodcurdling scream)*

Scene Three

Las Vegas, today. A rehearsal room at Caesars Palace. Two chorus boys, ZACK and P.J., enter in rehearsal clothes.

ZACK: Hey, don't be nervous, man. Mellow out.

P.J.: Mellow out? Easier said than done. I'm swallowing razor blades. You'd think I'd never been a chorus gypsy before. It's this town that's giving me the jitters.

ZACK: P.J., you're gonna love Las Vegas. It's the greatest place on earth.

P.J.: Besides Transylvania.

ZACK: What do you mean by that?

P.J.: Haven't you read in the papers about the string of vampire attacks on the Vegas strip?

ZACK: Who hasn't? But hell, why should you worry? All the victims were young girls.

P.J.: Vampires drink the blood of young virgins, right? As the song goes, "Take Me Back to Manhattan."

ZACK: Don't let this vampire thing get you down. Hey, give me a Vegas floorshow any day over some tired Broadway trip. And this isn't any ordinary floorshow. Do you know what the name Madeleine Andrews spells?

P.J. *(spelling it out):* M-A-D . . .

ZACK: No, doofus, it spells class. She's one hell of a lady.

P.J.: But she hasn't made a movie since the sixties.

ZACK: She did a TV movie two years ago where she played an insane millionairess who owns the Bermuda triangle and steals the shroud of Turin. It cleaned up in the Neilsons. Don't spread this around, but she may be starring in a Broadway revival of "The Sound of Music." Play your cards right and you may be employed for a long, long time.

(DANNY *enters*)

ZACK: But take this tip, buddy, stay away from the queens in this company.

DANNY: I heard that, Miss Zack. Stay away from the queens, indeed. Sweetie, has Miss Thing invited you to her dungeon room? Or did I arrive too soon?

ZACK: Fuck off, Mary.

P.J.: Hey guys, come on. Miss Andrews will be here any minute.

DANNY: I hope she is. It's about time she discovered this one's true colors.

ZACK: Jealousy, jealousy, jealousy.

DANNY: If you're referring to the one night we slept together, I'd talk about your cock, but I've got respect for the dead.

ZACK: You goddamn. . . . (ZACK *tries to attack* DANNY *but* P.J. *stops them*)

P.J.: Hey guys, come on, can't you discuss this calmly?

DANNY: I'll tell you what's going on. I've been dancing in Madeleine Andrews' Vegas act for five years. Before that I was a dancer on her T.V. Variety Show. I've paid my dues with that broad. My lover David has been with her just as long. Then Mata Hari here joins the company and tries to turn her against us.

ZACK: First we have vampires on the strip, now I've got an hysterical faggot to deal with.

DANNY: I wouldn't be worried about vampires, Whorina. Your ass is hardly virgin territory.

ZACK: Don't give me your beads. Your boyfriend's a drunk, he missed a show and Madeleine fired him.

DANNY: You didn't have to squeal on him.

ZACK: Boo hoo.

P.J.: Shh, Madeleine's going to hear you!

(MADELEINE ANDREWS *enters. It is of course* ASTARTÉ, *now the epitome of the glacial, terrifying star of stage, screen, video and Vegas*)

MADELEINE: Hello boys, ready to throw the old girl around? It's nice to see everyone on time for a change.

ZACK: Madeleine, this is P.J., the new dancer.

P.J.: It's a real thrill working with you, Miss Andrews.

MADELEINE: Call me Madeleine or we'll never get along. I love my boys and my boys love me, but there is one thing I will not tolerate and that is drinking or drugs. Is that clear?

P.J.: Yes, Miss Andrews.

MADELEINE *(laughingly):* I told you to call me Madeleine. *(Slaps him)* You're cute. Danny, aren't you going to say good morning?

DANNY: Is that quite necessary, Madeleine?

MADELEINE: You bet your sweet ass it is. Now Danny, I'm sure you're very upset that I was forced to fire David, but where this show is concerned, I am ruthless. It's my reputation on the line. If Caesars Palace is willing to fork over fifty smackers a week, I better damn well be worth it and that goes for everyone in this clambake. Got me?

EVERYONE: Yes, Madeleine.

MADELEINE: I detest being a boss lady. It's so unattractive. Danny, I'm very fond of you, I'd like to give you some good advice. You're better off without him.

DANNY: Madeleine, I don't want to sound rude but . . .

MADELEINE: Listen to Mama. You want to be a star?

DANNY *(sullenly):* Yeah.

MADELEINE: Take this advice. You can't have it all. A long time ago, I made up my mind that there were certain things I had to give up on the road to fame. One of those things was personal happiness. Well, let's get to work. I want this new number in by tomorrow night. Think we can do it, Zack?

ZACK: You bet.

MADELEINE: I hope so. I'll freak if I have to go onstage one more time and do that "I Will Survive" medley. Freddie, put on the playback.

(They do a strenuous dance number. CHARWOMAN *enters mopping the floor. It is the* CONDESA *fallen on hard times)*

MADELEINE: Cut! Cut! Cut! Zack, would you tell the cleaning lady we're rehearsing.

ZACK *(to the* CONDESA*):* Miss, excuse me. We're rehearsing in here. You'll have to come back later.

LA CONDESA: Look bub, I take my orders from Sol Weisenbloom.

ZACK: You don't understand. Madeleine Andrews is rehearsing.

LA CONDESA: Look kid, if I don't get this floor done, my ass will be in a sling.

MADELEINE: Perhaps I can be of some assistance. I'm Madeleine Andrews. (MADELEINE *walks over to the* CONDESA, *recognizes her and screams in shock)*

ZACK: Madeleine, are you all right? You look as if you've seen a ghost.

MADELEINE *(trying to compose herself):* I believe I have. Zack, I'm not quite ready to rehearse.

ZACK: Sure, Madeleine. Whatever you say. Hey guys, let's go get a coke. *(The boys exit)* We'll be just outside.

MADELEINE *(with great phoniness):* Zack, I love you. (ZACK *exits)*

LA CONDESA: La Astarté, as I live and breathe. Looks like you're in the chips.

MADELEINE: Can't complain. But what happened to your fortune?

LA CONDESA: Bad investments.

MADELEINE: What brings you here to Vegas?

LA CONDESA: Showgirls. You know I was always a sucker for a shapely gam.

MADELEINE: You've certainly been indiscreet. You've given the Vegas press vampires on the brain.

LA CONDESA: What, have you suddenly switched to artificial plasma? With you it's always the same tune, I'm the monster, you're the victim. My head reels when I think what you did to the girl scout troupe in forty-two. You bounced Hitler off the front page that week.

MADELEINE: Scandal rags. I learned my lesson from that one. Never again will I jeopardize my career. Now when I look for virgins I drive my Jaguar beyond the city limits.

(TRACY, *a very perky blond aspiring singer enters)*

TRACY: Madeleine, are you busy?

LA CONDESA: Oh don't mind me, come right in. Are you a new addition to Madeleine's act?

TRACY: Oh, I hope so. I'm Madeleine's latest protegée.

LA CONDESA: Wherever did you two meet? Here in Vegas or beyond the city limits?

TRACY: Oh right here in Vegas. I've been on tour with the Young Republican First Christian College Revue.

MADELEINE: Tracy, what is it you wanted to ask me?

TRACY: Which song do you think would be better for me to sing in your act, "I Enjoy Being a Girl" or "I Hate Men"? And also, how long do I sing before you bite my neck?

LA CONDESA: Please explain that bit of choreography.

TRACY: It's a special Halloween extravaganza. Madeleine appears as a glamorous lady vampire and . . .

LA CONDESA: I get the general idea. Madeleine, considering all the vampire business in the news, don't you think this could be construed as being in bad taste?

MADELEINE: Darling, she may have a point, let's keep that part of the act to ourselves. Kind of like a surprise.

TRACY: Sure thing. Well, I'll let you get back to your rehearsal. Tootles. (TRACY *exits*)

LA CONDESA: You lousy hyocrite. My blood simmers with hatred for you.

MADELEINE: You're just full of venom, aren't you? Look at your face in the glass. For two thousand years you've worn the same expression. Do you know what that is? You're smelling shit. You always look like you're smelling shit. Everywhere you go, you smell shit. Lady, that's your problem. My kind always smells the roses.

LA CONDESA: You don't smell too many roses in Siberia.

MADELEINE: What are you flapping your gums about?

LA CONDESA: 1952. You convinced me to take over your tour of "I Remember Mama." When we got to the Soviet Union, you had me arrested as a CIA spy.

MADELEINE: I never.

LA CONDESA: You did. While you were starting a new career in the movies, I was freezing my ass off in that Gulag.

MADELEINE: 1964. I was top contender for the Oscar. Nick the Greek had me winning ten to one, yet I lost it. Don't think I don't know it was you who spread those filthy rumors that I was boffing Mahalia Jackson.

LA CONDESA: Honey, you got it all wrong. You're the one who's been persecuting me. Me! You've been obsessed with me for two thousand years!

MADELEINE *(with intense emotion):* Yes, I'm obsessed with you. You made me what I am. Do you think I can ever forgive you for turning me into this, this thing that has no human feeling, this creature who thinks of nothing but her own survival, clawing and attacking anyone who poses a threat to me? Yes, I'm at the top of my profession, but I'm not so damn proud of it.

LA CONDESA: Excuse me, but I've got a floor to clean.

MADELEINE: Last year, Liv Ullmann and I toured Africa for UNICEF. While I was in the Congo, I left Liv one day and visited a tribal witch doctor named Pooji Dung.

LA CONDESA *(alarmed):* Pooji Dung?

MADELEINE: I see the name is familiar. He comes from an ancient line of jungle sorcerers. La Condesa, he has taught me all I need to know to destroy you.

LA CONDESA: So what do you expect me to do, scream, run around in circles? Do it, get out your voodoo dolls. This modern world stinks. Broadway's dead. You can't get a decent bialy. I've had it. Give me the jungle phase—out. You'll be doing me a favor.

MADELEINE *(chanting):*
Neemy Tunka Seevy Ra.
Keemy Funga Lami Ga.

LA CONDESA: But let me say this. When I'm gone, then will you be happy?

MADELEINE: Feemy, feemy, feemy ragoola. Eemana, eemana, Koorary, ragu . . . ragu . . . *(on the verge of hysteria)* Seemy nagu . . . *(collapses to the floor)* I can't! I can't kill you! Then I shall be truly alone. I've shed a tear. I feel something. Is it impossible that in this whole world, there is only you with whom I can travel through time?

LA CONDESA *(tough):* Save it for Valentines Day.

MADELEINE *(simply):* I need you.

LA CONDESA *(touched):* You need me. Someone needs me?

MADELEINE: In an odd way, your presence has always been a comfort.

LA CONDESA *(in reverie):* You need me. I am needed.

MADELEINE: Isn't that what life's all about? Funny. *(Trying to compose herself)* I'd better get back to rehearsal. What will you do now?

LA CONDESA: I hear at the All Souls Mission they're handing out free grub.

MADELEINE: Surely, you don't mean . . . Is there anything I can do?

LA CONDESA: Nah.

MADELEINE: No, really. Anything. Anything I can do, ten dollars, a warm coat.

LA CONDESA: Yeah, sure. I'd like to have one more shot at stardom. What can I say, I'm crazy for show business.

MADELEINE: Then my girl, you shall be in show business.

LA CONDESA: A comeback?

MADELEINE: A spectacular comeback. Let me give that to you.

LA CONDESA: But it's been so long. I haven't done anything since "Love American Style" in sixty-seven. I'd be terrified.

MADELEINE: We'll do an act together and we'll break it in in Tahoe. From there we'll hit San Francisco, Los Angeles, Chicago, Boston, the Kennedy Center and then Broadway!

LA CONDESA: Oh boy, the two of us singing and dancing up a storm. And we won't even think about the past.

MADELEINE: What past? At this moment we're the youngest chorines in town.

LA CONDESA: One more thing, dear, a small detail and something that really should be handled by lawyers and not us, nothing to get in the way of our deep friendship. But how do you see my billing in the act?

MADELEINE *(laughing at the irony of it all):* Dear heart, I can see it all. Glittering letters thirty feet high. Tonight on the great stage, Madeleine Andrews, Magda Legerdemain, the legendary, the notorious, love 'em or hate 'em, the Vampire Lesbians of Sodom!

(The two ladies explode in laughter. The music swells covering their enthusiastic voices as they begin rehearsing a dance step for their new act)

THE END